Killer Kids
Volume One

22 Shocking
True Murder Cases

Robert Keller

**Please Leave Your Review of This Book At
http://bit.ly/kellerbooks**

ISBN-13: 978-1987546835

ISBN-10: 1987546830

© 2018 by Robert Keller

robertkellerauthor.com

Table of Contents

Kim Edwards & Lucas Markham

It started with a slap, delivered by Elizabeth Edwards to her 6-year-old daughter Kim during an argument over which TV show to watch. Elizabeth immediately regretted lashing out and felt so badly about it that she reported herself to social services. That resulted in her daughters, Kim and Katie, being taken away from her for a time and placed in state care. The girls would be returned to their mother's home in Spalding, England, within months. But while Katie seemed unaffected by the brief separation and soon rebuilt the bond with her mother, Kim appeared to harbor a grudge, one that would grow into full-blown hatred over the next eight years; one that would lead eventually to a brutal double homicide.

Kim Edwards was an unusual child who, even as a pre-teen, seemed to view herself as an outsider. She was resentful of the relationship that her mother had with younger sister Katie, one that she believed showed favoritism and left her on the outside looking in. In truth, it was Kim who kept her mother (and the rest of the world) at arm's length. In September 2013, Elizabeth Edwards asked teachers at her daughter's school to keep an especially vigilant eye on the eleven-year-old as she had threatened to run away from home. Eight months later, Kim told a social worker that her mother had tried to strangle her, a claim denied by Elizabeth and disproved by a medical examination.

In January 2015, a teacher at Kim's school alerted Elizabeth to the fact that Kim had written her a letter in which she'd spoken of suicide. "I have tried to remain strong," the letter read, "but I can't fight any more. Now I feel that death is the only way." Concerned, Elizabeth spoke to her GP and asked him to arrange counseling for Kim. The subsequent sessions led the therapist to conclude that there was no indication of mental illness.

Then, in September of 2015, there appeared at last to be a chink of light in Kim Edwards's self-imposed darkness. It came in the form of 14-year-old Lucas Markham, a student at her school. Elizabeth was initially uncertain about the relationship, but at least Kim was smiling again. Even the strained interactions between mother and daughter seemed to improve. All too soon, however, Elizabeth's fears would be realized. Lucas was a surly and petulant youth, a delinquent and a trouble maker with a precocious interest in sex. Soon his bad influence would rub off on Kim.

In October 2015, after one of his frequent clashes with the school authorities, Lucas was given detention and decided instead to run away from home. Kim did not need much persuading to join him, and the pair departed that same afternoon, leaving town on their bicycles and carrying with them a tent, clothes, food, and other supplies. They would remain at large for five days during which a search was launched. The police eventually tracked them to some woods between the villages of Cowbit and Crowland. Thereafter, Elizabeth forbade her daughter from seeing Lucas, but she might as well have been talking to herself. Kim was beyond her control by now.

In March 2016, Kim ended up spending two days in hospital after an apparent suicide attempt. Then, on April 9, she got into another furious row with her mother after which she decamped to Lucas's house. There, the two of them barricaded themselves in Lucas's bedroom, resisting all attempts by Elizabeth and by Lucas's aunt to talk them out. Eventually, they escaped through a window. Just days later, while they were eating hamburgers at McDonald's, Kim raised the possibility of killing her mother. She'd suggested it, she'd later claim, as a joke. It was a joke that would soon turn deadly.

Just after midnight on April 13, 2016, Kim Edwards heard three closely spaced knocks on the window of the room she shared with her sister Katie. This was a pre-arranged signal, and Kim had been lying awake, eagerly waiting for it. She immediately slipped out of bed, padded on bare feet to the adjacent bathroom and opened the window. Lucas, standing in the darkness beyond, said nothing, instead handing Kim a sports bag. Something inside rattled as she placed it on the bathroom floor. Then Lucas was climbing through the window, and then he was inside.

The couple exchanged a brief embrace. No words were spoken and none were required since they'd discussed the plan in detail in the days leading up to this moment. Now they walked the short distance to Elizabeth's bedroom with Kim in the lead until they reached the door. Then she stood aside while Lucas placed his bag on the floor, crouched beside it and began rummaging inside. When he stood up again, he was holding a large kitchen knife.

Elizabeth Edwards was fast asleep when the first blow was struck, the cold steel of the blade biting into her throat and severing her windpipe. Despite this horrible wound, she instinctively fought back, grappling with her attacker as he straddled her. But Lucas was in a frenzy, delivering eight vicious blows in rapid succession. Five of those connected with Elizabeth's hands, slicing through flesh and tendons as she fought vainly to defend herself. But two thrusts of the knife got through and penetrated her neck, severing arteries and sending sprays of blood onto the walls and bedding. Standing in the doorway, Kim heard "gurgling sounds" coming from her mother. Then those sounds were extinguished as Lucas took a pillow and pressed it down on the stricken woman's face, holding it there until Elizabeth stopped moving.

Phase one of the deadly murder plot was complete. Now it was time for Kim to kill her 13-year-old sister, an act she'd been sure she could carry out. At the last moment, however, she shirked, telling Lucas that she could not go through with it. It was left to Lucas to knife the innocent child to death as she slept. Kim, standing in the hall outside their shared bedroom, heard her sister utter the words, "Get off me," and "I can't...." Then there was silence and moments later Lucas emerged from the room holding the bloody knife.

It was a horrific double homicide, made all the more so because of the tender ages of the perpetrators and the fact that the victims were the mother and sister of one of them. But what the teenaged killers did next was arguably even worse. As her mother and sister lay hacked to death in their beds, Kim Edwards led her juvenile lover to the bathroom where they shared a bath, gently sponging the blood from each other's bodies. Afterwards they went downstairs where they ate ice cream while watching a marathon of all five Twilight movies, breaking off periodically to have sex.

Kim and Lucas would remain in their macabre love nest for the next eighteen hours, even as the slaughtered bodies lay upstairs. During that time, members of the Edwards family became concerned that they were unable to reach Elizabeth by phone and called on the house. But their knocks went unanswered, and after three separate attempts, they went to the police. By then, Lucas Markham's aunt had also reported him missing.

Officers were dispatched to the house on April 15, arriving to find it securely locked. Getting no response when they knocked, they forced their way in, uncertain of what they'd find. What they did find was Kim and Lucas sitting under a duvet in front of the TV. Asked about Elizabeth and Katie, Lucas tartly informed them: "Why don't you look upstairs?"

Both Kim Edwards and Lucas Markham were charged with murder. Not that either of them was denying it. Edwards, in particular, left officers stunned with her cold demeanor. "I did it because I did not like Mum at all and I did not want her to ruin or corrupt anyone else," she said. "I did not feel anything for my mother, she deserved it and I'm glad she's dead."

The next day, Edwards made full admissions to police, giving a step-by-step account of the murders and their planning. Although she denied carrying out the actual killings, she insisted that Markham had carried them out with her full agreement. "We made sure we were both definitely, like, okay with it," she said. "He continuously asked me if I still wanted to go through with it and I said yes."

Edwards would carry that attitude with her into her trial, where she and her co-accused pled not guilty to murder but guilty to manslaughter. In Edwards's case, her counsel cited "an abnormality of mental function which impaired her ability to form rational judgments" as the reason for her plea. That, however, was rejected by the jury who found both defendants guilty.

Kim Edwards and Lucas Markham were each sentenced to life in prison with at least 20 years to be served before they are eligible for parole. The minimum term was later reduced to 17 years on appeal. That means that the so-called "Twilight Killers" could be back on the streets by their early thirties, a frightening prospect when you consider that the prosecutor likened them to the Moors Murderers, Ian Brady and Myra Hindley.

Eric Smith

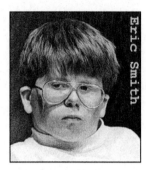

Derrick Robie was a happy kid, an active and fun-loving four-year-old who lived with his parents and younger brother in the tiny village of Savona, in western New York state. He loved tee-ball and riding his bike and standing on the sidewalk waving at cars as they passed by. He also liked hanging out with his friends, especially at the day camp that was held at a park a block from his home during the summer of 1993. His mom, Doreen, was happy to let him participate in the program. After all, it was supervised and safe and close by, the perfect environment for Derrick to interact with kids his own age.

During that summer, Mrs. Robie and her son had developed a routine. She'd pack a snack into his lunch bag and then walk with him to the end of the drive. From there, it was a short walk to the park, and she was able to watch him all the way until he reached his destination. On the morning of August 2, however, Doreen had her hands full. Her younger son, Dalton, was playing up and Derrick was getting impatient, insisting that he knew the route and could walk to the day camp on his own. Eventually, Doreen gave in to his nagging and sent him on his way with a kiss. The park was just a block away. There were no streets to cross. The walk should have taken him no more than five minutes.

Except that Derrick never made it. When his mother arrived to pick him up at 11:00, she learned that he hadn't arrived that morning. Then the police were called, and a frantic search was launched involving officers and civilian volunteers. It was tragically resolved four hours later when the toddler's brutalized corpse was found among a small copse of trees, halfway between the park and his home.

This was no ordinary killing but a murder of extreme savagery. Derrick Robie had been throttled into submission before rocks were dropped on his head, cracking open his skull. The killer had then rummaged through the child's lunch bag, taken out the flask of Kool-Aid he was carrying, and poured it into the head wounds. He had also, for some reason, smashed a banana that Derrick had in his bag. Then he'd pulled down the toddler's shorts and sodomized him with a stick. Finally, he'd posed the tiny corpse, removing the boy's sneakers and positioning one of them next to each of his hands.

It was a savage and sickening murder, made worse because the police suspected from the start that a juvenile killer might be responsible. The odd rituals performed at the crime scene certainly pointed to an immature mind.

Still, investigators had very little to go on. There were few forensic clues at the scene and no one had seen Derrick walking along the route that morning. Neither had anyone spotted anything untoward, a stranger in the neighborhood or someone who might potentially be the killer. The investigation, in fact, was going nowhere until an unexpected break, four days after the murder.

That was the day that a 13-year-old boy named Eric Smith walked into a police station, accompanied by his father, and said that he wanted to help with the inquiry. Smith was ushered into an interview room, but initially he appeared to have nothing to share. He admitted that he'd been attending the day camp but denied knowing Derrick Robie or having seen him on the morning he was killed. Then he abruptly changed the story, now saying that he had seen the boy, standing in the open field a short distance from the park. He then went further, accurately describing the clothes the toddler had been wearing and even the lunch bag he'd been carrying. A detective then asked Smith to describe the place where he'd last seen Derrick, whereupon the 13-year-old formed his hands into fists and started shaking. "You think I killed him, don't you?" he said in a breaking voice. The officer assured him that he didn't think that at all. He did, however, think that Smith might have seen something that would be useful to the investigation.

The following day, investigators asked Eric Smith to show them where he'd been standing when he'd last seen Derrick. Smith took up a spot over the road from the field where the boy's body had been found. He was calm, investigators noted, and he appeared almost excited as he shared his information. That was when alarm bells started jangling. The detectives were fully aware that killers often seek to insert themselves into police investigations. Was that why Smith had come forward in the first place?

Smith's family certainly thought that Eric knew more than he was telling. They urged him to be honest and tell the police what he knew. Seven days after the murder and two days after Derrick Robie had been laid to rest, Eric Smith finally admitted the dreadful truth. It was he who had waylaid the toddler on his way to the park, he who had persuaded the boy to follow him into the woods, he who had strangled him and crushed his skull with a rock.

Smith would provide no reason as to why he had so savagely slain a little boy who he did not even know. However, there would be plenty of theories presented at his trial. The jury heard that Smith had been prone to temper tantrums as a child and often banged his head against the floor. He had speech problems and learning disabilities and was held back at school. His red-hair, thick eyeglasses and protruding ears made him a constant target for bullies. He had no friends and would often spend hours riding alone on his bike.

As he grew older, Smith's anger management problems intensified to the extent that he would punch walls and trees until his knuckles bled. "It was literally deadly rage and anger," a defense psychiatrist testified. "After the episode, he'd appear entirely normal, but in that moment it was beyond his control."

Was this the deadly rage that Smith had unleashed on the little boy who had been unfortunate enough to cross his path? The defense seemed to think so but their evidence was refuted by the prosecution who pointed to a barrage of tests which had found nothing abnormal about Eric Smith's brain. According to the prosecutor, Smith had been tired of been bullied and had decided to hit back, targeting a child who had no chance of defending himself.

Ultimately, it was the prosecution's version of events that prevailed. On August 16, 1994, Smith was convicted of second-degree murder and sentenced to the maximum term available for juvenile killers – nine years to life in prison. The first three years of that sentence were completed in a juvenile facility before Smith was placed at a young offender's institute. Then, in 2001, he was transferred to the Clinton Correctional Facility in Dannemora, New York, one of the state's toughest prisons. He currently resides at Collins Correctional Facility, a medium security prison.

Smith has come up for parole nine times since completing his mandatory nine-year term and has been refused each time. While incarcerated, he has written a letter to the Robie family, expressing remorse for what he did to their son:

"I know my actions have caused a terrible loss in the Robie family, and for that, I am truly sorry. I've tried to think as much as possible about what Derrick will never experience: his 16th birthday, Christmas, owning his own house, graduating, going to college, getting married, his first child. If I could go back in time, I would switch places with Derrick and endure all the pain I've caused him. If it meant that he would go on living, I'd switch places, but I can't."

To Dale and Doreen Robie, who lost their precious little boy in such horrendous circumstances, those must sound like very empty words indeed. The Robies remain firmly committed to opposing any parole application lodged by Eric Smith.

Cayetano Santos Godino

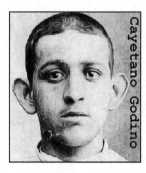

Compared to other Latin American countries, Argentina has produced relatively few serial killers. But one that the country did produce, Cayetano Santos Godino, must rank among the most malevolent murderers ever. Like the American "Boy Fiend" Jesse Pomeroy, this juvenile monster appears to have existed for one purpose only, inflicting pain on those weaker than him.

Cayetano Santos Godino was born in Buenos Aires, Argentina on October 31, 1896, the youngest of 10 children. His parents were poverty stricken, his father an alcoholic musician who was afflicted with syphilis at the time of Cayetano's birth, passing the effects of that dreaded disease on to his son.

Aside from this inherited affliction, Cayetano appears to have begun life with numerous strikes against him. He was a sickly child, on several occasions almost dying from poor hygiene and from enteritis, a sickness caused by consuming contaminated food. As if that wasn't enough, he was often subjected to brutal beatings by his father and older brothers. And then there was his bizarre physical appearance. Godino was a frail boy, with a small head and large protruding ears. He also had arms that appeared too long for his body.

Behavioral problems surfaced early in Cayetano Godino's life. Entering school at age five, he was soon expelled for disruptive behavior. His parents then moved him to another school and then another, each one declaring him impossible to control and asking his parents to remove him. Eventually, they gave up, leaving the boy to wander the streets doing as he pleased. And what pleased Godino most was hurting other children.

Godino's first documented assault occurred on September 28, 1904. On that day, he lured 2-year-old Miguel de Pauoli to a field with the promise of candy. Once there, he threw the toddler into a ditch filled with thorny bushes. Fortunately, a policeman heard the child's cries and came to his rescue, taking Godino into custody. He was released with a warning.

Encouraged by his escape, Godino waited just a week before he struck again. This time, he persuaded 18-month-old Ana Neri to follow him into a meadow. He then attacked the child, striking her on the head with a rock. Again a policeman intervened and again Godino escaped with nothing more than a reprimand.

Over the next 18 months, there were no other reported cases of
violence committed by Godino, although given his malicious
nature, he is unlikely to have remained inactive during this time.
Then, on March 22, 1906, a 2-year-old girl named Maria went
missing from the neighborhood. The girl's body was never found,
and Godino was not initially linked to the disappearance. Years
later, he'd admit that he'd led the little girl to some wasteland
where he'd attempted to strangle her. When that didn't work, he'd
tossed her into a ditch and filled it in with rubble, burying her
alive. By the time of his confession, a house had been built on the
burial site, so the police were unable to verify his account. If what
Godino said is true (and there is little reason to disbelieve him),
he'd committed his first murder at the age of 9.

A few days after the murder, Godino's father woke to find a
shoebox next to his bed. Inside were the family's pet canaries, all
of them strangled and with their eyes poked out. Enraged at what
the boy had done, his father marched him off to the local police
station and insisted that they take him into custody. They agreed,
shipping him to a reformatory for two months. By the time he
returned to his family, he'd developed a new vice, chronic
masturbation.

On September 9, 1908, Godino encountered 2-year-old Severino
Gonzalez playing unattended and coaxed the boy into a
warehouse. There he pushed the toddler's head into a horse
trough and attempted to drown him. He might well have
succeeded had the owner of the business not arrived to interrupt

him. With criminal cunning typical of killers of his ilk, Godino quickly concocted a story. He said that Severino had been brought to the warehouse by a "woman in black," and that he (Godino) had followed them and intervened when the woman tried to hurt the boy. Not only was this ludicrous story believed, but Godino was actually praised by the police for his bravery.

Six days after "saving" Severino Gonzalez, Godino attacked another child, burning 22-month-old Jolio Botle's eyelids with a cigarette. He ran off when the child's screams attracted its mother but the woman recognized him and reported him to the authorities. As a result, Godino was convicted of assault and shipped off to a juvenile facility called the "Colony of Smaller Peace," where he'd remain for the next three years.

Despite its name, the "Colony" was a brutal institution where Godino suffered physical and emotional abuse. He tried to escape several times, each time being hauled back to complete his sentence. By the time he was released on December 23, 1911, Godino had just turned 15. Rather than curing him of his afflictions, the Colony had hardened him. He was about to enter the most murderous phase of his criminal career.

Godino had discovered a couple of new vices while he was inside. One of them was alcohol. The other was more deadly – arson. His neighborhood was soon afflicted by a number of unexplained blazes as two houses, a factory, a stockyard, and a railway station went up in flames. Godino would later admit that he enjoyed lurking in the shadows to watch the results of his handiwork. "I like to see the firemen at work," he said. "It's nice to see how they fall into the fire."

On January 21, 1912, the body of 13-year-old Arturo Laurora was found in an abandoned house, beaten and strangled to death. Again, no one suspected Godino, although he'd later confess. He said that he'd taken the boy to the house, gagged him with a handkerchief and then started beating him with a tree branch. When he grew tired of that game, he strangled Arturo, leaving his body behind to be discovered.

On March 7 of that year, a 5-year-old girl named Reyna Vainicoff was looking at some shoes in a store window when she suddenly started screaming, and onlookers were astounded to see that her dress was ablaze. A policeman went to her aid, throwing himself on the girl and extinguishing the fire. However, the child was so badly burnt that she died in hospital 16 days later. Cayetano Godino had claimed his third victim.

On November 8, Godino lured Russo Roberts, aged 2, to a warehouse with the promise of candy. He tried to strangle the boy with his belt but, when interrupted, trotted out his old story about saving the toddler from a mysterious woman. Amazingly, the police again believed his story. The child's parents even gave him a reward.

But Godino's bloodlust was growing, driving him to take ever more outrageous risks. He started attacking children on busy streets in broad daylight. Several times, he was chased off by adults, who passed on his description to the police. Given his distinctive appearance, it wasn't hard for the police to pin these attacks on Godino, known to them as the "Jug-eared Dwarf." Yet they didn't arrest him, choosing instead to keep him under "loose surveillance," hoping to catch him in the act. This ill-advised approach would have a tragic impact on another child.

On the morning of December 3, 1912, Godino encountered his neighbor's son, 3-year-old Jesual Giordano, playing outside his house. Godino knew the boy, so it was easy to persuade him to go for a walk. However, rather than walking with Jesual to the local candy store, as promised, Godino took him to a vacant building. There he bound the boy's hands and feet and began strangling him with a rope. Jesual, though, put up such a fight that Godino gave up his attempt at strangulation, deciding instead to bludgeon the child to death.

Leaving the building to hunt for a weapon, Godino soon encountered Jesual's frantic father, searching for his son. The man came rushing up to Godino and asked if he'd seen the boy. Godino said he hadn't. He then waited until Mr. Giordano was out of sight before picking out a suitably sized rock. He found something else too, which he thought might be useful, a rusty 9-inch nail. With unspeakable malice, Godino then returned to the child and used the rock to pound the spike through his forehead. He then covered Jesual's body with a sheet of corrugated iron and walked home.

Jesual's father, meanwhile, had reported his son's disappearance to the police, and it didn't take long before they found a witness who had seen the boy walking with Godino. That led officers to the building where Mr. Giordano had encountered Godino. They found the little boy's corpse inside and Godino was soon in custody.

Godino was still under age at the time of his arrest, so he was ordered to be confined to a reformatory. There, he was examined by doctors who ruled that he was insane and recommended his transfer to a mental institution. The trial judge, however, refused, and thus Godino remained at the reformatory until November 1915, when the judge's ruling was finally overturned.

After spending eight years in a mental hospital, Godino was transfer to Ushuaia Penitentiary in 1923. On November 15, 1944, he was found dead in his cell, apparently from internal bleeding caused by gastritis. That, at least, was the story given by the authorities. The unofficial word was that Godino had been beaten to death by fellow inmates.

Connor & Brandon Doran & Simon Evans

Connor Doran Brandon Doran Simon Evans

Anyone who knew the Doran brothers around the Walton area of Liverpool, England, knew that they were trouble. Connor and Brandon, aged just 16 and 14 respectively, were given free rein by their mother, Linda. They could be found wandering the streets at all hours, creeping through neighbors' gardens, usually up to no good. Any reprimand from an adult was met with a smirk or a few choice words. At Walton High School, which they seldom attended, they were known as poor students and frequent troublemakers. Recently, they had taken to boasting to classmates about the exploits of their older brother Ryan. Twenty-three-year-old Ryan Doran was awaiting trial for murder, after he beat a man to death with his fists and a beer bottle.

And there were even more serious incidents involving the brothers. Recently, Connor had been picked up by police after making threats of violence against a local storekeeper. The incident occurred after Connor's girlfriend was caught shoplifting and the storekeeper decided to call the police. Then Connor threatened that if the man did not let his girlfriend go, he'd return with a gang of machete-wielding youths and "hack him to pieces." The storekeeper called the police anyway, and both Connor and the girl were arrested. Charges were still pending.

Simon Evans was fourteen years old when he first met Connor Doran in August 2012. By all accounts, he was a well-behaved boy who achieved good grades and was described by teachers as a model student. But all of that was to change after he started hanging out with Connor. Then, suddenly, he was skipping classes and getting into mischief. Soon he'd far exceed anything that could be described as "mischief." Soon he'd be involved in a murder.

On the night of Friday, August 17, 2012, Connor Doran and Simon Evans were hanging out together. Also in their company that evening was Connor's younger brother Brandon, who Simon had met for the first time that day. The trio had nothing in particular to do and no place in particular to be, but just before midnight, they decided to walk down to a shop on County Road to buy some energy drinks.

At around the time that the teenagers set off on that mission, a 52-year-old man named Kevin Bennett was just staggering out of a local pub. Bennett was a well-liked man around the area, even if he had recently fallen on hard times and was living on the streets. He was a heavy drinker who spent virtually all of his dole money on booze. On the night in question, he'd consumed as many as twelve cans of lager. He was carrying a shopping bag laden with more cans of beer as he shuffled along County Road in the direction of one of his usual sleeping spots, the back lot of a local supermarket. It was just as he settled down for the night that the boys found him.

Later, there would be conflicting testimony as to who had initiated the attack. According to Simon Evans, it was Connor Doran who first spotted Bennett and then challenged Evans to kick him. "Do you fancy doing him in with me?" Doran is alleged to have said. "If you kick him first, I'll do the rest." Evans went on to say that Doran had been in an "aggressive mood" that night and that he had been afraid to disobey him. He'd therefore kicked the sleeping man and Doran had then waded in on him. Brandon Doran had not participated in the attack but had run to the corner of the building to act as a lookout. By the time the teenagers fled the scene a few minutes later, Kevin Bennett had suffered a savage beating.

Bennett was found at around 7 a.m. the following morning by supermarket staff. He was rushed to hospital where it was found that he had suffered a collapsed lung, several broken ribs and a fractured eye socket. Nonetheless, he was expected to survive.

The police, meanwhile, had begun investigating the vicious assault, beginning with CCTV footage from the supermarket's security cameras. The area where the attack had occurred was unfortunately not covered. But detectives were able to pick up the three attackers as they appeared around the front of the building. There, they stopped for a moment, and one of them crouched down in front of the other and appeared to be examining his trouser legs (for blood spatters, the police believed). Then, the three figures disappeared into the night.

The evidence looked promising at first but proved to be of little help. The attackers' faces were hidden behind hoodies, and no amount of enhancement would improve the grainy film. That was a setback for the investigation, but the police were about to get a major break in the case. A woman named Evans reported that her son had confessed to her his involvement in the beating of a homeless man behind the Iceland supermarket on County Road. Simon Evans was then brought in for questioning and soon gave up the names of his accomplices.

But bringing in the Doran boys proved to be more difficult than expected. When the police first arrived at their residence, their mother laid low and did not open the door. Later, when officers eventually got to speak to the boys, Linda Doran provided them with an alibi, saying that they had been at home all night. She later retracted that statement when confronted with the CCTV footage. By then, the charge was far more serious than common assault. Kevin Bennett had developed complications due to his injuries and had died six days after the attack. This was now a case of murder.

Connor Doran, Brandon Doran, and Simon Evans appeared at the Liverpool Crown Court in February 2013, charged with murder.

All three were found guilty. Identified as the ring leader, Connor was sentenced to life in prison with a minimum of 12 years. Simon Evans got eight years for his secondary role in the murder while Brandon got four years. Linda Doran, who had provided her sons with a false alibi, was later convicted of defeating the ends of justice and sentenced to 31 months behind bars.

Jessica Holtmeyer

The quiet, rural town of Clearfield sits slap bang in the middle of Pennsylvania, in an area that was once sustained by the logging industry. Those halcyon days, however, have long since moved on, taking with them the jobs once on offer to the townsfolk. Many have upped sticks and moved north to Pittsburgh, about an hour's drive away. To those that remain, in particular the younger generation, that move often remains an unrealized ambition.

Jessica Holtmeyer would certainly have counted herself among those planning to get out of Clearfield as soon as the getting was good. In fact, the frumpy, heavyset teen spoke often of jacking a car and heading for Florida. And she had a ready audience to nod in agreement at her ambitious plans. Jessica was the de facto leader of a loosely affiliated gang of miscreants who spent most of their time hanging out and getting drunk. She wasn't the oldest or the biggest of the group, but she was known to be loud and aggressive and quick to meet any challenge with violence. The others knew well enough not to push their luck. Even the oldest of the group, 24-year-old Tracy Lewis, deferred to Jessica. Clint Canaway 17, Patrick Luccas 16, Teresa Wolfe 14, Dawn Lanager 14, and Jessica's boyfriend, Aaron Straw, 18, followed suit.

But Tracy, nonetheless, played an important role in the collective. Her job, as the only adult, was to buy booze for the rest of them. And perhaps it was this special role that motivated Jessica to cut Tracy some slack. When Tracy's mentally challenged cousin, Kimberly Jo Dotts (known as Kimmy), arrived in town to stay with family, Jessica allowed her to hang out with them. Short and overweight, the 15-year-old Kimmy soon became the butt of all the gang's jokes. She appeared to take it all in good humor, but perhaps she was quietly seething at the abuse because eventually she took revenge. She ratted Tracy out to her aunt for buying booze for minors. When the aunt threatened to go to the cops if Tracy continued to do so, the gang's supply of beer was effectively cut off.

Jessica, surprisingly, appeared to take this betrayal with good grace. She had more important things on her mind, she told her followers. She'd eventually found someone who would drive them all to Florida in his minivan. Plans were thus hatched, plans that included Kimmy, who had apparently been forgiven for her transgression. On the frigid morning of Sunday, May 10, 1998, the group met up at a local hunting resort to raid the cabins for whatever they could steal before they set off for their new life in the Sunshine State.

The pickings were slim that morning, although the gang were delighted to find several bottles of booze and also a length of rope. Then someone mentioned the fact that the area they were in was called Gallows Harbor and that it had been the site of judicial executions in the 1700s and 1800s. From there, it was a short hop to a deadly challenge. Each of the gang members was encouraged to stand on a box with a noose around their neck, a test of loyalty, as Jessica called it.

All went well until Kimmy stepped onto the box. Then, as the 15-year-old grinned down trustingly at her supposed friends, Jessica yelled, "Yank it!" and the other gang members pulled hard on the rope, elevating Kimmy off the ground. As the teenager clawed frantically at the noose that was biting into her throat, and kicked desperately at the vacant space beneath her feet, Jessica shouted out the order to lower her to the ground. But the respite was brief. Crying, gagging, gasping for air, Kimmy was hoisted back up. When she was lowered to the ground this time, she had gone limp.

"Is she breathing?" somebody asked, to which someone else replied, "Yeah." But whatever spark was left in Kimmy's body would only be of short duration. Jessica picked up a basketball sized rock and carried it over. "Fucking snitch," she hissed as she dropped it on Kimmy's head. The sound was akin to fine China being crushed under a boot heel.

The gang was surprisingly calm in the aftermath of this atrocity. Even Tracy Lewis, who had just seen her cousin brutally slain before her eyes, followed Jessica's directions to cover the body with brush. Then the group hitchhiked back to Clearfield to hook up with their Florida ride. It was there that Jessica informed them that she and Aaron were no longer going. The others decided to make the trip anyway, but were soon returned to Clearfield after they were picked up by Florida State troopers and found to be underage. In the meantime, Kimmy had been reported missing and a police search was underway to find her.

Kimberly Jo Dotts was discovered a few days later in the woods near Gallows Harbor. As she'd been found outside of the city limits, jurisdiction for the murder inquiry fell under the Pennsylvania State Police, which was bad news for Jessica and her cohorts. The Staties were much better equipped to run the investigation than the Clearfield police department, and they were determined to bring the killer of a mentally impaired teenager to justice.

That, as it turned out, proved to be a relatively simple task. Kimmy had last been seen in the company of the Holtmeyer crew, and they were quickly hauled in for questioning. Surprisingly, it was Jessica who cracked first. She did not admit directly to the murder but said that she often suffered blackouts when she got excited and may have done so in the grip of such an episode. Along with the forensic evidence the police had already gathered, it was enough to bring charges.

Legally, Aaron Straw and Tracy Lewis were the only adults among the group. But the decision was made early on to try Jessica as an adult too, while the others were charged as juveniles. In court, the rest of the gang quickly turned on Jessica, saying that she had intimidated them and that they feared for their lives if they dared to disobey one of her orders.

With that evidence stacking up against her, Jessica never stood a chance. She was found guilty and sentenced to life in prison without parole. As the ruling was read, the tough-as-nails Jessica did something that no one had ever seen her do before, she started crying and continued sobbing uncontrollably as she was led away to begin her sentence.

Jessica Holtmeyer is currently incarcerated at the woman's prison in Muncy, Pennsylvania. Of her co-accused, Aaron Straw was also sentenced to life without parole, while Tracy Lewis got 20 years. The younger members of the group were sentenced to juvenile detention.

Ricky Kasso

Everyone in Northport, Long Island knew that Ricky Kasso was crazy. The 17-year-old 'Acid King' had done so much LSD, smoked so much Angel Dust, that it had turned his brain to jelly. When he was high, he'd walk deep into the Aztakea Woods, outside of town, to converse with Satan. He said that the Devil appeared to him as a glowing tree. On other occasions, he went to the local cemetery to smoke up. He'd recently been arrested for digging up a corpse. No, you didn't want to mess with crazy Ricky. Gary Lauwers found that out the hard way.

Gary and Ricky had been friends, fellow dustheads who enjoyed getting stoned together. That was until Rick passed out at a party and Gary rifled through his pockets and stole ten bags of Angel Dust. Problem was that he'd done so in front of witnesses. When Ricky later confronted him, he returned five of the little yellow envelopes that contained the drugs. He promised to pay for the other, the five he'd used, but he was slow in doing so. Bad mistake. Bad, bad, bad mistake.

At first, Ricky resorted to standard intimidation methods. He tracked Gary down and, along with his friends, Jimmy Toriano and Albert Quinones, beat him senseless. When that didn't work, he repeated the remedy – three more times. Eventually, he threatened to kill Gary if he did not come up with the money. It was a threat that Gary took seriously. Soon after, he began telling friends that Ricky was going to murder him. He started carrying a hunting knife for protection. He also began making a concerted effort to scrape together the fifty bucks that he owed. Eventually, he handed it over, leading to Ricky calling a truce. "What's a few bags of dust compared to a good friend?" he told Gary.

On the evening of June 16, 1984, Ricky Kasso, dressed in an AC/DC t-shirt, was trawling the streets of Northport with Jimmy Toriano and Albert Quinones, pushing drugs to his teenaged clientele. And there were plenty of those around; school had only recently let out. The Northport teens were in the mood to party.

One of those out on the town that night was Gary Lauwers. Earlier in the evening, Gary had visited a female friend and told her of his plans to quit drugs, finish school and eventually go to college. By the time he encountered Kasso, Toriano, and Quinones, however, Gary was high as a kite. When Kasso suggested they go into the Aztakea woods to smoke some dust, he readily agreed. After all, had Ricky not forgiven him for his earlier transgression, had he not paid back the 50 bucks, were he and Ricky not friends?

We know what happened in the woods that night only because of the testimony of Albert Quinones, who agreed to testify against his co-accused at the subsequent trial. According to Quinones's version of events, the foursome had walked deep into the woods to find a spot to get high. Once they located a suitable place, they took a few hits of the mescaline that Kasso had brought along, then decided to build a fire. At this stage, Ricky and Gary were talking and laughing together, just like the friends they'd always been.

With a pile of logs and kindling gathered for the fire, Ricky tried to get a blaze going. But the wood was damp due to recent rains and wouldn't ignite. Gary then took off his socks and set them alight, succeeding briefly in getting a small blaze started.

This, however, did not last long. As the flame died, Ricky, in a more menacing tone, suggested that Gary burn the denim jacket he was wearing. "How about I just use the sleeves?" Gary said, removing the jacket. He then produced his hunting knife and hacked the sleeves from the jacket, set them alight and got a small fire blazing. But this, too, was soon reduced to embers, and Ricky then suggested that Gary cut off some of his hair and throw it on the fire.

The tension now, despite the drugs they'd taken, was obvious. Gary got slowly to his feet, seemingly ready to flee at any moment. "I have funny vibes that you're going to kill me," he said.

"What?" Ricky responded. "Are you crazy? I'm not going to kill you."

And perhaps, up until that moment, he hadn't really considered killing Gary. Perhaps Gary's premonition was what actually triggered the attack. Whatever the case, Ricky suddenly launched himself at his friend. He was bigger and stronger, given additional strength by the mescaline he'd taken. Still, Gary put up a valiant fight. As they rolled on the ground, he broke free and made a run for it, gaining a few yards before Jimmy Toriano tackled him to the ground. Then Kasso was on top of him, using his teeth to tear at his victim, ripping a chunk of flesh from his throat, severing an earlobe. Meanwhile, Toriano joined the attack, using his boots on Gary's ribs.

Still, Kasso wasn't done. Retrieving Gary's hunting knife from the ground, he began stabbing him, inflicting several deep wounds. Then he pulled his helpless victim to his feet. "Say you love Satan," Kasso demanded, speaking directly into Gary's bloodied face.

"I love my mother," Gary rasped, something that appeared to infuriate Kasso. He launched another attack with the knife, stabbing Gary again and again, inflicting a total of 32 wounds to his chest, neck and face. Eventually, he allowed his victim to slump to the forest floor.

But Lauwers was not yet dead, and neither was his suffering over. Before he eventually expired from his horrendous injuries, Kasso inflicted some more. Gary was burned, slashed across the face and had his eyes gouged. Death, when it came, must have seemed like a mercy. Kasso and Toriano then dragged the body deeper into the woods, covered it with leaves and walked away.

In the aftermath of the murder, Kasso and Toriano fled to Saratoga Springs, fearing arrest. They needn't have worried. Gary Lauwers was a habitual runaway, and his friends and family assumed that he'd hit the road again. No one reported him missing. The only other person who knew about the murder was Albert Quinones, and he was hardly about to rat out his buddies. In fact, when Kasso phoned him a couple of days later, Quinones told him that there was no heat at all over Gary's disappearance and that it was safe to return to Northport.

Had Rick Kasso been able to keep his mouth shut, he might well have gotten away with murder. But the Acid King was never likely to do that. Keen to impress his teenaged hangers-on, he began boasting about the murder he'd committed, "in the name of Satan." He even added some embellishments, insisting that he'd heard a crow caw at the moment that Gary Lauwers died. This he took to be a sign from Satan, giving his approval for the murder.

It was a tale that Kasso told several times over the weeks that followed. If anyone expressed doubts about his story, he'd invite them into the woods to view Gary's decomposing remains. A number of Northport teenagers took him up on that offer, tramping deep into the Aztakea to satisfy their morbid interest. And yet, remarkably, not one of them went to the authorities. It was only when a friend of Gary's heard the stories via the grapevine that the truth came out.

After receiving an anonymous tip, the police sent canine units into the Aztakea woods on July 4, 1984. It wasn't long before the dogs picked up a scent and led their handlers to the badly decomposed corpse. The notches clearly visible on the exposed ribcage left no doubt as to how he'd died.

Ricky Kasso, Jimmy Toriano and Albert Quinones were taken into custody on July 5. Under questioning, Kasso had no problem admitting to the murder. In fact, he did so in such an upbeat tone that investigators should perhaps have been concerned about his state of mind. He should probably have been placed on suicide watch. Instead, he was returned to his cell where, on July 7, 2004, he hanged himself. His co-accused, Jimmy Toriano, was later acquitted of second-degree murder.

The aftermath of Gary Lauwers's murder brought forth wild speculation about its occult connections. This was after all the eighties and "Satanic panic" was at its height in America. Was Ricky Kasso really inspired to kill by his satanic beliefs? It's doubtful. The only connection that could be found to any devil-worshipping activities was a loose affiliation with the so-called 'Knights of the Black Circle,' a bunch of high school kids involved in séances and animal sacrifice. There was also speculation that Kasso was influenced by his love of Heavy Metal music, especially the 'satanic' lyrics of his favorite band, AC/DC. This is unlikely, since the only 'satanic' references in the band's repertoire appear to be tongue-in-cheek swipes at those accusing them of writing satanically influenced material.

The truth is that Ricky Kasso was the classic case of a young life lost to addiction. He'd once been a bright student and a talented athlete, but his involvement with drugs had put an end to that. It had also led him down the path to murder.

Alex and Derek King

In the early morning hours of November 26, 2001, residents of Cantonment, a small community about ten miles north of Pensacola, Florida, were alerted by the strident wails of sirens. A couple of fire trucks raced by, heading in the direction of Muscogee Road, an area that the firefighters knew had mainly old, wood-framed houses. They were concerned that if a blaze took hold in the neighborhood, it would quickly spark a major conflagration.

Bringing their vehicles to a stop outside the burning building, the firefighters quickly went through their well-drilled preparations to begin extinguishing the blaze. That was when a neighbor approached and said that he believed someone was trapped inside the house. A couple of firemen then entered, breaking down the dead-bolted front door to gain access, and then working through the house in a search for survivors. It was in the living room that they found the man, sitting on a couch with blood clotted around a

head wound. And it was immediately clear that he was not a victim
of smoke or fire. His skull was cracked open and his face had been
beaten to a pulp. This man had been murdered.

The victim was soon identified as 40-year-old Terry King who,
according to neighbors, had been living in the house with his 12-
year-old son, Alex, since the previous summer. Over the past few
weeks, another son, Derek, had also been living at the address.
Derek was 13 years old.

But where were the boys now? And had they been somehow
involved in their father's death? Lead investigator, Detective John
Sanderson, didn't know the answer to those questions. However,
as he was soon to find out, Derek and Alex were troubled little
boys who had endured a lot of hurt in their short lives.

Derek and Alex were the children of murder victim Terry King and
his partner Kelly. The couple had met in 1985, and although they
had never married, they had stayed together for eight years during
which time Kelly had given birth to the boys. The relationship,
however, was troubled, and during one of their many breakups,
Kelly fell pregnant by another man, eventually giving birth to twin
boys. A short while after, she abandoned all four of her children
with Terry and hit the road. Unable to cope, Terry placed them in
the Heritage Christian Academy. Within a year, the twins had been
adopted, and Derek and Alex had been placed with separate foster
families.

Fostering did not work out well for the King brothers since they had poor social skills and were prone to destructive behavior. The younger boy, Alex, lasted less than a year before his placement was canceled and he was returned to the care of his father. Derek, meanwhile, had been living with the family of Frank Lay, a high school principal who no doubt thought that his unique skill set would help him get through to the troubled boy. And in all fairness, the Lay family did try. Eventually, though, Derek's disruptive behavior, his glue sniffing, and especially his love of starting fires, became too much for them. He returned to live with his father on September 25, 2001 and that sparked a drastic change in the dynamic of the King household.

Up until now, Alex had appeared happy living with Terry, but he soon fell under the influence of his older brother. Derek was openly hostile towards his father. He resented his rules and responded aggressively to any attempt at applying them. Music, in particular, seemed to stir him up, forcing Terry to eventually remove the stereo and TV from the home. Derek's response was to persuade Alex to run away with him. That was on November 16, ten days before Terry King showed up dead. Now, a search was underway for the missing boys.

That search would not endure for long. On November 27, a family friend, Rick Chavis, brought the boys into a police station and told stunned officers that they wanted to confess to the murder of their father. Derek and Alex were then taken to separate interview rooms, where they told essentially the same story.

According to their confessions, it had been Alex's idea to kill their father, but it was Derek who had wielded the bat. Derek said that they had entered the house while their father was asleep. They'd crept into his bedroom and Alex had hit him with an aluminum baseball bat, inflicting at least ten blows to his head and face. They'd then dragged him into the lounge and propped him up on the couch before setting the house on fire and fleeing. They'd done it, they said, because they feared being punished for running away. They also admitted that their father had never beaten them, although he sometimes punished them by making them sit in a chair while he stared at them. They told investigators that they found this punishment mentally abusive.

Derek and Alex were both charged with murder and placed in a juvenile detention center. Then Detective Sanderson got to work resolving another mystery. Where had the boys been during the ten days between running away from home and the murder? The evidence kept leading Sanderson back to the same name, Rick Chavis. It would soon emerge that Chavis was far more than just a family friend. He was a pedophile who had been carrying on a sexual relationship with Alex King. That offense saw him charged with lewd and lascivious assault on a minor. He was also charged as an accessory after the fact to murder.

On December 11, 2001, a Florida grand jury indicted both boys, making them the youngest murder defendants in the state's history. Florida law stipulates that anyone charged with a homicide is automatically tried as an adult, regardless of age. If found guilty, the boys faced mandatory life sentences.

But the King case was about to take a dramatic turn. In April 2002, the boys testified before another grand jury, and this time they had a different story to tell. They now insisted that it had been Rick Chavis who had killed their father. According to this revised story, Chavis had wanted the boys to come and live with him but had told them that their father would never allow it. (Terry King had, in fact, warned Chavis to stay away from his sons shortly before he was killed). Chavis had then told the boys that the only way they could be together was if their father was dead. On the night of the murder, he'd driven them to their father's house and had told them to wait in the car while he went inside. A short while later, he'd returned and told them that he had murdered their father and set the house on fire. Then he drove them away from the scene.

Immediately after the boys told their story, Rick Chavis was indicted on first-degree murder, evidence tampering, and sexual battery of a child. At his subsequent trial, he vigorously denied the boys' claims that he had murdered their father. For their part, Derek and Alex remained mostly true to their story, although they did waver on some of the details. Derek, in particular, seemed evasive, now claiming that he couldn't remember certain events. Several other witnesses, including the Lay family, testified that Derek had spoken openly about killing his father. In the end, it took the jury just five hours to reach their decision.

The trial came to a suspenseful end when the judge announced that the verdict would be sealed until Alex and Derek King had been given their day in court. That day came around in September 2002 and covered much of the same ground as the Chavis trial. This time, the jury took two-and-a-half days before finding the King brothers guilty of second-degree murder and sentencing each of them to life plus 30 years. The judge then read the Chavis verdict. He was acquitted on the murder and arson charges.

But the King case still had a few twists and turns to offer up. In October, a judge overturned the convictions. Then comedian Rosie O'Donnell entered the fray and hired two high-powered lawyers to represent the boys at the retrial. In the meantime, the matter had gone to mediation and a deal was eventually struck whereby the brothers were allowed to plead to third-degree murder. The prison terms this time were far more lenient – eight years for Derek and seven for Alex, with credit for time served.

Alex King was released from prison in April 2008, his brother in March 2009. Rick Chavis, acquitted on child molestation charges but convicted as an accessory to murder and for evidence tampering, remains behind bars.

Barry Loukaitis

Barry Dale Loukaitis was born on February 26, 1981. He spent the early part of his life in Iowa and Minnesota before his family relocated to Washington State when he was in the fifth grade. His parents, Terry and Jo Ann, operated a sandwich shop together at Moses Lake, but theirs was a far from happy marriage. Jo Ann was a dominant woman who sought to control her husband and was an overbearing presence in her son's life. That led to friction in the home, with Terry and Jo Ann constantly at each other's throats, arguing so viciously that all Barry could do was to take refuge in his room.

And the situation was made even worse in 1995, when Jo Ann found out that Terry was having an affair. Thereafter, the family home was turned into a virtual war zone until Terry eventually moved out. Then Jo Ann began plotting a gruesome revenge. Her plan was to drive to the house that her estranged husband now shared with his new lover, tie them up, and then commit suicide in front of them. The date for this bizarre pact was to be Valentine's Day 1996. Incidentally, she suggested that Barry might have to kill himself at the same time.

And so Barry's home situation was far from ideal. But if the boy thought that he might find some respite at school, he was sorely mistaken. A sensitive child who suffered from hyperactivity and had been prescribed Ritalin, he was a target for bullies. He was regularly beaten up, had his head dunked in toilets and, on one occasion at least, he was held down by a group of students while another urinated on him. One particular nemesis was a boy named Manuel Vela who regularly taunted and humiliated him. Lately, Vela had resorted to calling him a "fag" to the amusement of his other tormentors.

How did Barry Loukaitis respond to this? In much the same way as put-upon kids the world over. He tried to keep his head down and fly under the radar, he retreated to the sanctuary of his room, he constructed impotent revenge fantasies, supplementing them with violent reading and viewing material. A favorite book was the Stephen King novel, Rage, in which a student takes his algebra class hostage and shoots two of his teachers. Movie fare included the Leonardo DiCaprio film, The Baseball Diaries. In it, a teenager fantasizes about gunning down his entire class. Barry had a favorite song too, Jeremy by Pearl Jam. It is about a set-upon boy who takes revenge against bullies in a school shooting spree. It is easy to see a theme developing here.

Just what it was that shifted 14-year-old Barry Loukatis's revenge fantasies into nightmare reality is not known. There is evidence to suggest that the abuse by his nemesis, Manuel Vela, had increased over the preceding weeks, and there was also the pressure of his mother's threatened suicide. Barry had begged her not to go through with it, but it appeared that JoAnn was determined. And that date was fast approaching. Twelve days before it was due to happen, Barry trumped his mother by carrying out a shooting spree of his own.

On the morning of Friday, February 2, 1996, Loukaitis arrived at Frontier Junior High School wearing a strange getup. He was dressed all in black and wearing a long black coat, a "duster" similar to the type favored by Western outlaws. The duster had a specific purpose. It concealed the .30 caliber hunting rifle he was carrying. Also in Loukatis's possession that day were two handguns – a .357 pistol and .25 caliber semiautomatic – and 78 rounds of ammunition.

Math teacher Leona Caires was giving an algebra class when Loukaitis entered the room, raised the rifle and shot her in the chest, killing her instantly. "This sure beats algebra, doesn't it?" he said as he turned the weapon on his classmates. Manuel Vela, Loukatis's old foe was the first to die, gunned down where he sat. Then, as the other students started screaming and scuttling for cover, Loukaitis fired again, killing 14-year-old Arnold Fritz. A third shot struck and severely wounded Natalie Hintz, although she would survive her injuries. Loukaitis then hustled the terrified students into a corner of the classroom where he held them at gunpoint.

The commotion, of course, had not gone unnoticed. Down the hall, gym teacher Jon Lane had heard the shots and the screams and responded immediately. He entered the classroom and approached Loukatis, urging him to put down the rifle and let the students go. Loukaitis responded that he needed a hostage so that he could leave the school safely. Lane then volunteered to be that hostage and Loukaitis agreed, allowing the terrified students to leave the room. But Loukaitis had miscalculated badly. Lane was a former champion wrestler, and he soon managed to wrench the rifle from the boy's grasp and subdue him. In the meanwhile, the police had been summoned, and they arrived minutes later to take Loukaitis into custody.

Barry Loukaitis was brought to trial before the courts in Seattle, Washington, in August 1997, the trial having been moved there due to extensive coverage in the media. By then, the decision had already been made to try him as an adult, meaning that the now 16-year-old Loukaitis faced the possibility of life in prison without the possibility of parole.

Since there was very little doubt as to the facts of the case, Loukaitis's defense attorney, Joan Petrich, opted for an insanity plea, claiming that mood swings were the cause of Loukaitis's violent actions. According to Petrich, Loukaitis had experienced "delusional and messianic" thoughts before the shooting. "He felt like he was God and was superior to other people," she said. "Then those feelings were replaced by hate, disdain, and not measuring up."

This defense might well have had merit given the history of clinical depression that ran through both Loukaitis's paternal and maternal bloodlines, going back at least three generations. But Barry's admission that he had intended to gun down his enemy, Manuel Vela, and that he'd shot the other victims when "reflex took over," hurt his defense. It allowed the prosecution to argue that he'd carefully planned the shooting and had come to school that day with murder in mind. Hardly the actions of someone who was insane.

In the end, it took the jury a full four days of deliberations before they returned with their verdict. On September 24, 1997, Barry Loukaitis was convicted of two counts of first-degree murder, one count of second-degree murder, one count of first-degree attempted murder, and 16 counts of aggravated kidnapping. He was sentenced to serve two life sentences and an additional 205 years without the possibility of parole.

Barry Loukaitis is currently imprisoned at the Clallam Bay Corrections Center in Washington State. He will remain behind bars for the rest of his natural life.

Tylar Witt & Steven Colver

Tylar Witt was a typically rebellious teenager. A freshman at Oak Ridge High School in El Dorado Hills, California, the pretty 14-year-old was into emo Goth-style clothing, Japanese anime, and MySpace. She was often to be found hanging out at the Habit coffee shop in El Dorado, with a bunch of teens who shared similar interests.

Home life for Tylar was far from ideal. The only child of a single mother with whom she often clashed, Tylar had run away on several occasions. As a young child, she'd once been removed from her mother's custody, when Joanne Witt was still afflicted with a drinking problem. These days, Joanne had her demons under control, but her rebellious daughter was another matter. Tylar might have given up on running away, but she was still a handful. These days she'd taken to directing her frustrations inward, inflicting self-harm with razor blades.

Around January 2009, Steven Colver, a 19-year-old who had recently graduated from Tylar's school, began hanging around at Habits. He and Tylar struck up a friendship, with Colver filling the "big brother" role, offering advice and guidance. They began talking regularly on the phone, with Tylar confiding the details of her difficult relationship with her mother. The platonic relationship evolved quickly, and by March 2009, the two had slept together for the first time. Tylar was a virgin at the time and was instantly besotted, noting in her diary, "We will love each other past death. I know I will never stop loving him."

In April 2009, a series of events occurred that would deepen the relationship between Tylar and Colver and also set in motion a tragic chain of events. Steven Colver's father decided to move out of state, meaning that Steven needed a place to stay. At the same time, Joanne Witt was looking to rent out a spare room in her house. Seizing on the opportunity, Tylar suggested to her mother that she rent the room to her friend, Steven. Joanne was at first hesitant to bring an older teenager into the home but eventually relented after Tylar told her that Steven was gay. Colver moved into the Witt home in April 2009, paying rent of $500 per month.

For the first few weeks, the arrangement worked wonderfully. The ultra-polite Colver helped with chores around the house and often interceded on Joanne's behalf when Tylar acted out. He even offered to tutor Tylar at math and e-mailed her teacher to get her assignments. To Joanne, Steven Colver must have seemed like a godsend. She, of course, didn't see the stolen kisses, much less what went on when she was out of the house. It took only six weeks before the illusion was shattered.

On May 13, 2009, Joanne found a bottle of sexual lubricant, various sex toys, and a stash of marijuana in the house. Not wanting to believe that the objects belonged to Tylar, she confronted Steven. He readily admitted that the stash was his, but insisted that he was only holding it for a friend. He was calm and unerringly polite, and Joanne was convinced. Her initial instinct had been to ask him to move out, but she decided to let him stay. It was a move she'd come to regret almost immediately.

Just the next day, Joanne returned home unexpectedly. Not finding Tylar in her room, she walked down the hall to Colver's bedroom, intending to ask him if he knew where Tylar was. When she knocked on the door, she heard scurried movement. Colver didn't open the door for several minutes. When he did, he was wearing only his jeans. Sensing something amiss, Joanne pushed into the room and opened the closet, where she found Tylar naked, save for a yellow sports bra that she held clutched to her chest.

Joanne was shocked to discover that her 14-year-old daughter was having sex with her 19-year-old boarder. She spent the rest of the afternoon mulling over how to deal with the situation. Eventually, she asked Colver to take a drive with her to a local park where the two of them could talk things over. There, a contrite Colver admitted that he and Tylar had been sleeping together for over two months. Anxious to keep the matter out of the public eye,

Joanne agreed not to press charges of statutory rape, provided Colver moved out of the house immediately and stopped seeing Tylar. He agreed.

🞐 🞐 🞐

A few days after Stephen Colver moved out of the Witt home, Joanne had cause to go back on her word, when Tylar went missing. Convinced that she was with Colver, Joanne called the police and filed rape charges. Tylar, as it turned out, was with a female friend, but the damage was done. The police hauled the pair in for questioning about their relationship. They told a similar story, insisting that they were friends and nothing more. The incident where Joanne had found Tylar naked in Colver's room had been a misunderstanding, they said. Tylar had been there modeling clothes, not engaging in sex. In fact, Colver insisted that he was homosexual, even providing the name of a gay lover. Unable to break either of them under interrogation, the police were forced to let the matter drop.

The rape allegations served to further erode the relationship between Joanne Witt and her daughter. Tylar was angry at her mother for trying to have Colver charged with a criminal act. For her part, Joanne remained committed to exposing the truth about Colver's illicit relationship with Tylar. She found it in Tylar's diary, described in graphic detail. Also in the diary, Tylar opened up about her feelings towards her mother, including elaborate fantasies about Joanne dying in a car accident.

Those entries, the ones describing Tylar's feeling towards her, left Joanne in a quandary. She now had the evidence to put Steven Colver away, but she didn't want the police to read about her personal relationship with her daughter. She decided to have the police speak to Tylar one more time, to see if they could convince her to come clean about her sexual relationship with Colver. However, when El Dorado Sheriff's Deputy Ken Barber called on the Witt home on June 10, Tylar stuck to her story. Joanne then gave Barber the diary.

Tylar was outraged when she heard that her mother had handed her private diary over to the police. On the evening of June 11, 2009, she and Colver exchanged several phone calls. At around midnight, with Joanne having retired to bed, Colver showed up at the house. He spent the night in Tylar's bedroom. Sometime before daybreak on June 12, the lovers left the house together. They planned on traveling to San Francisco where they would commit suicide together in an ending worthy of Romeo and Juliet. First, though, they were going to spend the day in El Dorado Hills, saying goodbye to friends.

Joanne Witt did not show up for work on Friday, June 12, but her colleagues were not overly concerned. Joanne had skipped work before, usually when she had to deal with some crisis of her daughter's making. However, when she still hadn't shown on Monday, June 15, they reported the matter to the police and asked them to check on Joanne. When officers found the house locked and no one responding to the doorbell, Joanne's father, Norbert

Witt, was called. He arrived to allow the officers in. They were unprepared for what they found.

Joanne Witt lay on her bed in a pool of congealed blood, a gore-soaked Spongebob Squarepants blanket drawn over her. An autopsy would later reveal that she'd been stabbed 20 times in the neck and chest.

Steven Colver and Tylar Witt, meanwhile, had checked into a Holiday Inn in downtown San Francisco. They'd spent the weekend sightseeing, doing drugs and writing suicide notes, which they mailed to Matt Widman, Colver's friend and former lover. They then made a halfhearted attempt to follow through on their suicide pact. First, they tried ingesting rat poison but couldn't bring themselves to eat enough of the substance to cause actual harm. Next, they tried cutting their wrists, but Colver couldn't bear to inflict pain on himself. Finally, Colver suggested jumping off the hotel's roof, but Tylar said she couldn't do it, as she was afraid of heights.

Aware by now that the police were probably looking for them, Colver and Witt decided to head south, leaving San Francisco on foot on June 16. The following morning, they were spotted by a police officer in the town of San Bruno and placed under arrest.

⁇ ⁇ ⁇ ⁇

From the outset, it was decided that Tylar Witt would be tried as an adult. The evidence against both of the defendants was pretty solid, and a long prison term surely awaited. However, Witt's attorney was able to strike a deal. She'd testify against Colver in exchange for a reduced charge of second-degree murder and parole eligibility in 15 years. With that deal in place, prosecutors were confident that a conviction against Colver was a mere formality. It didn't turn out that way.

The Colver/Witt trial soon descended into a case of he said, she said. According to Tylar, Colver had planned the murder and wielded the knife. But Colver told a different story. He said that he'd arrived at the Witt residence to find Joanne Witt already dead and Tylar holding a bloody knife. All he was guilty of was covering up the crime.

In the end, it was up to the jury to decide, and they came down on the side of Tylar Witt. Steven Colver was found guilty of first-degree murder with aggravating circumstances and was sentenced to life in prison without the possibility of parole. Tylar Witt was found guilty of second-degree murder. Her sentence was 15 years to life.

Kip Kinkel

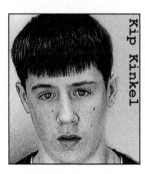

His parents were popular teachers at Springfield, Oregon's two high schools. His sister was a high school valedictorian and a college cheerleader who had won national honors. Yet Kipland "Kip" Kinkel had a far more dubious claim to fame. He was voted by his middle school classmates as "Most Likely to Start World War III."

It is easy to see where Kip Kinkel's reputation stemmed from. The freckle-faced 15-year-old had a fascination with guns; he'd once been arrested for dropping rocks on passing cars from an overpass; he frequently made outlandish statements, usually to the effect that it would be fun to kill someone. Not only that, but the boy was into bomb-making and often boasted about torturing and killing animals. As an English literature project, he'd once stood up in front of the class and read an essay about how he'd built a bomb using instructions downloaded from the internet and had used it to blow up a cow.

William and Faith Kinkel, Kip's parents, tried everything to help their troubled son, but despite their extensive experience as schoolteachers, nothing seemed to work. The boy's problems had been noticeable even before he'd started firstgrade. He was a difficult and defiant child, prone to temper tantrums when he did not get his own way. At school, he struggled academically, leading his parents to believe that he might be suffering from dyslexia or Attention Deficit Disorder. When tests for both proved negative, they tried helping him with his schoolwork and encouraging him to get involved in leisure pursuits. They took him camping, hiking, and sailing and signed him up for karate and football. Bill even gave up his teaching career and took early retirement in 1991, just so that he could spend more time with his son.

But, if anything, things got worse. When Kip started getting into fights at school, his parents took him to a private therapist who prescribed Ritalin, then Prozac, and then anger management classes. None of those produced any tangible result. Bill then took the extreme step of trying to channel Kip's interests into a more productive pursuit. He bought a Ruger .22 target pistol and a .22-caliber rifle and encouraged the boy to join a shooting club. Kip went to only one meet before he lost interest. Then he demanded a 9mm Glock pistol, which his father eventually gave in and bought for him. A short while later, a neighbor complained that Kip had been firing the pistol in the backyard, and Bill then put his foot down. He locked the guns away in a safe to which he had the only key. The weapons, however, remained in the home, a mistake that would result in tragedy.

On the morning of May 20, 1998, a teacher at Thurston High School got a tip-off that there was a .32 caliber Beretta pistol hidden in locker No. 781 – Kip Kinkel's locker. A search was carried out and the firearm was found just where the tipster had said it would be. Kinkel was then marched to the principal's office, where he was held until the police arrived. In the interim, William Kinkel was called and advised that his son had been suspended pending an inquiry and might end up being expelled. William, who had taught Spanish at Thurston High before his recent retirement, fully understood the school's position. He was furious at Kip for doing such a foolhardy thing.

But at least this latest infraction had brought matters to a head. Bill was tired of pussyfooting around his son. It was time for decisive action, and Bill knew exactly what he was going to do. He was positively upbeat when he played a game of tennis with a friend that afternoon. Shortly after he got home, Bill made the call he'd been thinking about, to the Oregon National Guard, to inquire about a summer boot camp they were running for wayward young men. He'd barely hung up the phone when Kip stepped up behind him, raised his semiautomatic Ruger rifle and pumped a single, fatal bullet into the back of his father's head.

Bill Kinkel was dead before he even realized he'd been shot. Then Kip dragged the body into the bathroom and sat down to await his mother's return from her teaching job. When Faith Kinkel stepped out of her car, she found her son standing before her in the garage. "I love you," he said, before raising the rifle and shooting her in the face.

Kip Kinkel, at the age of just 15, was now a double murderer. And he was only getting started. With his parents lying dead downstairs, he spent most of the evening building a series of bombs which he distributed around the house in various booby traps. Then he watched some television and went to bed. He had a big day ahead of him.

The next morning, May 21, Kip rose early and went through his usual routine of ablutions and breakfast. Then he dressed, supplementing his usual ensemble with a long fawn trench coat. Next, he loaded up his weapons, the 9mm Glock, .22 caliber Ruger and .22 rifle, each of then carrying a full clip. Additional magazines for the weapons were stuffed into a rucksack. A military hunting knife, strapped to his ankle, completed the arsenal. Happy with his preparations, Kip got into his mom's Ford Explorer and pointed it in the direction of Thurston High School.

Kinkel entered the school building just before 8 a.m. and headed directly for the cafeteria, which he knew would be buzzing at that hour. On route, he encountered a student who he advised: "You might want to get out of here." Moments later, he entered the canteen and almost immediately flipped back his trench coat to reveal the rifle. Before anyone even had time to cry out, he opened fire, working the room right to left and then back again, shattering a plate glass window and sparking a stampede of screaming kids.

Nineteen students were shot that day, two of them fatally. And the body count might have been much higher but for the bravery of one young man. Seventeen-year-old Jake Ryker, a school wrestling champion, had been shot in the hand and chest. But he did not hesitate to tackle Kinkel when Kinkel emptied his magazine and stopped to reload. Other male students then joined the fray, subduing and disarming Kinkel. By then, the police and paramedics were already on route, and before long, injured students would be rushed to McKenzie-Willamette Hospital. One of them, 17-year-old Mikael Nicholauson, was pronounced dead on arrival; another, 16-year-old Ben Walker, would die later of his injuries. Given that Kinkel had emptied a magazine of 50 rounds, it is a miracle that there were not more fatalities.

Kip Kinkel was hauled off for questioning and almost immediately suggested that the police search his parents' house. There, they found the corpses of Bill and Faith Kinkel, the parents who had sacrificed so much for their murderous son. Bill had been shot once in the head while Faith had suffered several wounds to head and abdomen. Each had been covered with a white sheet.

But Kinkel had not sent the police to his house just to find his murdered parents. He'd rigged the place with explosive devices, no doubt with the intention of causing further fatalities. One of the bombs did, in fact, detonate but it caused no harm. The others were defused by the bomb squad. Back at the station, Kinkel tried a more direct approach. He still had the hunting knife strapped to his ankle, and he used it to attack a detective. All he got for his trouble was a face-full of pepper spray.

Kinkel would ultimately be tried as an adult and found guilty on four counts of first-degree murder. On November 10, 1999, he was sentenced to 111 years in prison without parole. He is currently incarcerated at the Oregon State Correctional Institution in Salem, Oregon.

Jon Venables & Robert Thompson

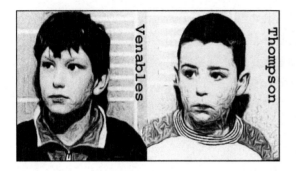

On Friday, February 12, 1993, Denise Bulger made a trip to the
Bootle Strand Shopping Center in Liverpool, England. With her
was her two-year-old son, James, a blue-eyed, cherub-faced
toddler, who was the apple of his mother's eye. Denise seldom
went anywhere without taking James along. On this particular day,
Denise had a couple of chores to run, but James was being difficult.
He refused to ride in his stroller and insisted on walking.
Fortunately, Denise had her brother's girlfriend, Nicola, along to
help with the hyperactive child.

That same day, two local delinquents named Jon Venables and
Robert Thompson were also at the mall. The two were playing
truant, as they often did, and as usual, they were up to no good.
They'd come to the shopping center to steal and had quickly
accumulated an assortment of shoplifted items, including
batteries, a tin of paint, pens and pencils, a troll doll, a wind-up toy

soldier, fruit and candy, woman's makeup, and other items. Most of what they took, they later discarded. They were stealing for fun, not for gain.

Shoplifting wasn't the only mischief the boys got up to that day. At a hardware store, they kicked at a can of paint until it started leaking; they were ejected from McDonald's for jumping on the chairs and tables; they tormented an elderly lady, continually running up behind her and pushing her in the back. They were told to leave by shop assistants and mall staff. They simply laughed off the warnings.

In the meantime, Denise Bulger had finished her shopping. She had one more stop to make, at the butcher shop. James was still playing up and, with Nicola shopping at another store, Denise made the fateful decision to leave him waiting at the door while she went inside. She'd only be a moment.

Jon Venables and Robert Thompson were standing at a concession stand near the butcher shop when they spotted the little boy in the blue anorak. Earlier in the day, they'd tried to lure another two-year-old and had been chased off by the child's mother. This child, though, appeared to be unattended.

It was Venables who approached the toddler. "Come on, baby," he said, holding out his hand. Innocently, James took it and followed the boys as they led him through the center and then outside. A surveillance camera caught them as they left, Venables still holding James by the hand, Thompson walking ahead. It was

3:42 p.m.

By now, Denise Bulger was involved in a frantic search for her son. Not finding him in the immediate area, she was directed to the security office where she provided a description of James and the clothes he was wearing – grey tracksuit, blue anorak, "Noddy" tee-shirt, blue wool scarf with a white cat face on it. The security officer told her not to worry. Children got lost in the center all the time. A quick announcement over the P.A. system and James would soon be back with her.

But no one responded to the announcement, and after another desperate search, Denise rushed to the Marsh Lane Police Station to report James missing. It was now 4:15 p.m. James had been gone for just over half an hour.

After Venables and Thompson left the shopping mall with James Bulger, they walked up Stanley Road. By now, the toddler was distressed, crying for his mother, but the boys ignored his pleas. At times they carried him, at other times they dragged him along. Eventually, they reached a canal and stopped at an isolated spot under a bridge. It was there that they first hurt James.

At first, they planned on pushing James into the canal and even tried to lure the child to the water's edge. But James was afraid, so one of them (they later blamed each other) picked James up by the legs, held him upside down and then dropped him on his head. As the child lay stunned on the hard cobbled surface, and then started wailing, they ran away. A few moments later, they returned and soothed the toddler. James had a cut and a large bruise on his forehead, but when Venables held out his hand, he innocently took it, and again followed his tormentors. Thompson then flipped the anorak hood over the child's head to hide the injuries.

After leaving the canal, the trio followed a meandering path, crossing Stanley Road and walking past shops, office buildings, parking lots. Many witnesses would later come forward to say that they'd seen the toddler with the tear-streaked face being led by the two older boys. Some even said that they saw the cut on James's forehead, saw the bigger boys pulling him along. A motorist said he saw one of them kick James in the ribs. Someone else said they saw Jon Venables punch James and shake him. And yet no one thought to intervene. Most would later say they thought the three were siblings. Others described James laughing as the older boys goofed off to crack him up.

As the boys sat by a reservoir, an elderly woman noticed James and saw that he was injured. When she approached Venables and Thompson, they said that they had found James "at the bottom of the hill." The woman told them to take him to the nearby Walton Lane Police Station and even gave them directions. But the boys ignored her, walking in the opposite direction. Inexplicably, the woman failed to report the incident to the police.

The boys had been walking for two miles now, ending up on County Road. There, they entered several shops, with James in tow. A number of adults queried them about James. Their story was invariably that they'd found him wandering around and were taking him to the police station. At one stage, Thompson, who was holding James by the hand, let him go. But then Venables nudged him and whispered urgently, "Get hold of his hand." The adults who witnessed this scenario thought it strange, but took no action.

Leaving the shops, the boys crossed heavy traffic onto Church Road West. There was a fire in one of the houses, and they stood for a while and watched it. Later, they encountered two older boys who knew Robert Thompson. The boys asked about James. Robert claimed he was Jon's little brother.

By the time they reached the railroad tracks, it was 5:30 p.m. and already dark. A decision now had to be made, what to do with James. The police station was close, but they were afraid to take James there. He had cuts and bruises, questions would be asked. Neither could they take the toddler to either of their homes. That would earn them a beating. There was a hole in the fence in front of them, an embankment leading down to the tracks. They decided to go there.

The murder of James Bulger occurred between 5:45 and 6:30 p.m. on Friday February 12, 1993. It began when either Venables or Thompson threw blue paint into James's face. The paint entered the toddler's eye, no doubt stinging him. He started to cry. At that stage Venables and Thompson started beating him, kicking him, stomping him (an imprint of Thompson's shoe was found on James's cheek). They threw bricks at the child, pulled off his shoes and pants, inserted batteries into his rectum, sexually molested him. Eventually, they clubbed him with an iron bar. Then, when they thought he was dead, they laid his tiny body across the railroad tracks and covered his head with bricks and stones.

After the inhuman attack on James Bulger, Venables and Thompson went to visit a friend. Finding that the boy wasn't home, they hung out at a local video store, which was where Susan Venables, Jon's mother, eventually found them. She'd been looking for Jon and was furious, beating both boys and then dragging Jon home.

By now, the disappearance of James Bulger was already receiving extensive coverage on the news. Almost immediately, the police were inundated with calls from people who claimed to have seen the toddler. But the most promising lead came from the surveillance footage at the shopping mall. Although the film wasn't clear enough to positively identify the perpetrators, it showed plainly that the abductors of James Bulger were children themselves.

The next morning, divers were sent to trawl the bottom of the canal, while dozens of police officers conducted a grid search, starting at the Bootle Strand and working outwards. They found no trace of the missing child.

James's body was found on Sunday afternoon by four boys playing near the railroad tracks. In the day and a half since Venables and Thompson had placed it there, it had been struck by a train and cut in half. The upper body was clothed, the lower, naked, lying some distance away. It would later be determined that James had suffered 42 injuries, mostly to his face and head. But he hadn't died during the initial beating. He'd still been alive when Venables and Thompson left him on the tracks. He'd died sometime between then and when the train had cleaved him in two.

Even experienced investigators were shocked at the brutality meted out to two-year-old James Bulger. As his mother received the terrible news of her son's death, the shocked community joined her in grief. The area close to the crime scene was flooded with flowers, cards and tributes. One of those was from Robert Thompson, who placed a single rose at the site.

Meanwhile, Jon Venables was following the case on television with an almost obsessive interest. At one stage, he told his mother, "If I see them lads, (the boys who'd taken James) I'll kick their heads in." Then, after his mother informed him that James's body had been found, he said, "His poor mum."

The search for the killers was by now well underway, with the police scouring school absentee lists and dozens of tips being called in, many by parents who suspected their own children. One of those calls came from an anonymous tipster who gave up the name Jon Venables. She said that Venables resembled the boy in the video, had skipped school on Friday, and had been seen with blue paint spattered on his jacket. She also mentioned that the other boy might be Robert Thompson, with whom Venables had played truant that day.

Venables and Thompson were brought in for questioning on Thursday, February 18. They were interrogated separately, Venables crying and hysterical, Thompson sullen and defiant. Both, however, denied having anything to do with James Bulger's murder. But as the police kept up the pressure, Venables eventually cracked, blurting out, "I killed the baby!" Then, after Thompson was informed of his friend's confession, he too, admitted involvement. Both boys, though, pointed to the other as the instigator and main aggressor.

Jon Venables and Robert Thompson went on trial for the murder of James Bulger at Preston Crown Court on November 1, 1993. Despite their earlier confessions and the overwhelming evidence against them – video footage, blood, fibers, footprints, paint spatters, eyewitness testimony – each denied abduction and murder. It was to no avail. On November 24, both Venables and Thompson were found guilty of murder, making them the U.K.'s youngest convicted killers of the 20th century. In his summation, the judge, Mr. Justice Morland, described the crime as "unparalleled in evil and barbarity."

Venables and Thompson were ordered detained "at Her Majesty's pleasure," but given their ages, that sentence would amount to just eight years behind bars. They were released in June 2001, both aged 18, and with a new identity and the guarantee of anonymity for life. That move has been broadly criticized, in particular, by the Bulger family.

Robert Thompson has kept a low profile since his release, but John Venables has been in and out of trouble with the law, most recently in February 2018, when he was convicted on child pornography charges and sentenced to three years in prison. Some of the children in the images found in his possession where as young as James Bulger.

Carl Newton Mahan

The town of Paintsville sits among steep hills in the coal mining belt of eastern Kentucky. It has never been a prosperous place, and it was far from prosperous in 1929, when our story takes place. The stock market crash that would usher in the Great Recession across America was still months away, but for the good folk of Paintsville, the hard times had already arrived. Hewing coal from a pit mine is a tough living at the best of times, especially when the mine owners paid such a pittance to the men doing the tough and dangerous work.

The coal miners of Kentucky are a hardy breed, accustomed to back-breaking work and crushing poverty. They make do with what they can earn by their own efforts, and that trait extends even to their children. Take Carl Mahan and Cecil Van Hoose, for example. Just six and eight years old respectively, the boys were already trying to make their way in the world, in their case by searching for scrap metal to sell. Thus it was that on the morning of May 18, 1929, they found themselves trudging up a hillside, casting around for rusty treasure.

The pickings had been decidedly slim that day until Carl spotted a large chunk of pig iron in the scrub grass. It was a valuable find, worth a few pennies at least from the local scrap dealer. Carl quickly unfurled the burlap bag he was carrying and prepared to load it up. That was when his older, bigger companion stepped up and snatched his prize away. Carl, of course, protested the theft, citing the "finders keepers" rule. But Cecil wasn't about to listen to his protests, not when there were a few valuable pennies involved. He delivered a swift slap to Carl's head to back him off. Then he snatched up the chunk of iron and walked away, cradling it like a baby.

But Cecil had made a grave mistake in stealing from his young companion. Even as he walked towards the scrap dealer to cash in his bounty, Carl was running downhill, towards the shack he shared with his parents and siblings. There, he pulled a chair towards the wall where his father's shotgun was racked. Standing on tiptoes, he removed the 12-gauge from its resting place. His father had already shown him how to use the weapon, and so he instinctively broke the breech and checked that there were shells loaded in the twin barrels. Happy that his weapon was armed, he set off in pursuit of his thieving friend. A short while later, he encountered Cecil in the street.

Bystanders who witnessed the incident would later testify that Carl made little effort to disguise his intentions. He simply shouted out: "I'm going to shoot you!" and then lifted the weapon and fired, hitting Cecil in the chest and spilling him to the dirt. The boy was dead before he hit the ground.

Justice moved swiftly back in those days, even for a 6-year-old who was the youngest ever homicide defendant in Kentucky's history. Less than a week after he shot Cecil Van Hoose, Carl Mahan found himself in front of a judge, charged with murder.

Carl made no effort to deny what he'd done. That would have been pointless anyway since the shooting had occurred in front of witnesses. And he made no pretense as to his motive. He'd intended to kill Cecil, he said, because Cecil had stolen from him. Then, after describing the events leading up to the shooting and the shooting itself, the skinny little kid with the cowlick put his head down on the defense table and promptly fell asleep. Looking at his angelic face, it was difficult to believe that this was a murder defendant.

The trial of 6-year-old Carl Mahan was a brief affair, concluding within the space of a single day. And the jury deliberations were shorter still. Within just 30 minutes, the foreman announced that they had reached their decision. Carl Mahan was found not guilty of murder but guilty of the lesser charge of manslaughter. The sentence of the court was that he be sent to a reform school for fifteen years. In the meanwhile, he was released into the custody of his parents on $500 bail.

But the trial and verdict had provoked furious debate in Johnson County, and already the battle lines were drawn. On the one side, there were those who believed that a six-year-old could not understand the implications of his actions and therefore should not have been convicted. They felt that the 15-year sentence was way too harsh. On the other, there were those who held that manslaughter was too lenient a charge and that Carl should have been convicted of murder and sentenced to life in prison. There were even less charitable souls who insisted that he should have been put to death in the electric chair.

In the end, though, all of those arguments were academic. Shortly after the conclusion of the trial, a Circuit Court judge issued a "writ of prohibition" blocking the state from sending Carl Mahan to reform school. A month later, Kentucky's attorney general set aside the conviction and sentence, allowing the boy to remain under his parents' supervision with no restrictions. Kentucky's youngest ever convicted murderer had escaped punishment entirely.

FOOTNOTE: Information about Carl Mahan's later life is sparse, although we do know that he later moved to Jefferson County and died there in 1958, at the age of 35.

Dedrick Owens

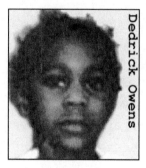

Even at the tender age of six, teachers at Theo J. Buell Elementary School knew that Dedrick Owens was trouble. The little boy was known to taunt and bully his first-grade classmates, punching, slapping and pinching them. Once he'd beaten a boy who had refused to give him a pickle from his lunchbox. On another occasion, he'd stabbed a little girl with a pencil. He also routinely peppered his speech with the "F" word and had been sanctioned for trying to kiss his female classmates. All of this had led to him being flagged under the Primary Mental Health Project, a national initiative aimed at identifying children with aggressive tendencies. He was scheduled to see a psychiatrist.

But not all of the blame for his destructive behavior could be laid at the little boy's feet. He'd hardly had the most auspicious start in life. Dedrick was born in Flint, Michigan, in 1993. His mother, Tamarla, was a shop assistant, while his father, Dedric Darnell

Owens, was a work-shy individual of no fixed employment other than the criminal kind. He would be behind bars for at least a third of his son's life, usually on drugs and theft charges. Inevitably, this put a strain on the marriage, and in March 1999, while Dedric was serving yet another jail term, Tamarla filed for divorce.

Single parenthood was not easy for Tamarla, especially with three children to feed and drug problems of her own to contend with. She worked two jobs, but the $250 she earned a week wasn't enough to cover her bills. Eventually, she fell into arrears with her rent and was evicted from her home. Tamarla then moved in with her sister, taking her 5-year-old daughter with her. Her two young sons were placed with their uncle, Marcus Winfrey, in Mount Morris Township, Michigan, at a property that was known to police as a crack house.

Life must have been difficult for the boys, just 6 and 8 years old respectively and placed in a situation with no parental care or adult supervision. Their junkie uncle certainly was not going to fulfill that role, and their mother barely bothered to visit them at the house on Juliah Avenue, a sparsely furnished hovel with flaking paint and cracked window panes. The boys were left mainly to their own devices and spent much of their time wandering the streets or sitting on the porch watching the steady stream of crackheads heading into and out of the property to shoot up. By night, they slept on a filthy mattress in the living room, their slumber interrupted by inebriated adults shooting up, quarreling or having sex.

Given this background, it is perhaps unsurprising that young Dedrick Owens was gaining such an unsavory reputation at the nearby Buell Elementary School. The boy was a handful to the teaching staff and a threat to his classmates with whom he was in constant conflict. His latest confrontation had been with a little girl named Kayla Rolland. Kayla was one of the girls who had refused Dedrick a kiss, and he had responded by spitting on her desk. The two then had a verbal exchange which was quickly broken up by a teacher. Dedrick, however, continued to harbor a grudge. On February 29, 2000, he arrived at school determined to make Kayla pay for challenging him.

Early on that Tuesday morning, a student alerted a teacher to the fact that Dedrick Owens was carrying a knife. The teacher then challenged Owens about the weapon, and he reluctantly handed it over. But what the teacher did not know was that the six-year-old had another weapon on his person, a fully loaded Davis .32 semi-automatic. This is a pocket-sized pistol, designed for easy concealment. Owens had found it in his uncle's room the previous night and had brought it to school with him, intent on using it.

Shortly before 10 a.m., the first-graders were heading upstairs for a computer-training class. Kayla was walking ahead of Owens on the stairs when he suddenly shoved her in the back and told her: "I don't like you." Kayla then turned and challenged him with a typically juvenile gesture. "So?" she pouted, hands on hips. It was then that Owens pulled the gun.

A single shot was fired, entering the six-year-old's abdomen under the armpit and chewing through vital organs on its path. Kayla grabbed her chest and collapsed to the floor gasping for air. A teacher, who was following close behind, ran forward, took one look at the little girl and immediately punched 911 into her cellphone. In the meantime, Owens had made a run for it. He was later found hiding in a restroom, the gun hidden in a trash can nearby. Kayla, meanwhile, was being given first aid by the paramedics who had arrived on the scene. She was rushed to Hurley Medical Center but was pronounced dead on arrival at 10:29 a.m.

In the aftermath of the shooting, the school principal ordered a lockdown of all classrooms. Soon the halls would be crawling with police officers and then, as word got out, with concerned parents arriving to take their children home. Dedrick Owens, of course, wasn't going home. He was taken to a nearby police station for questioning.

Owens at first tried to lie his way out of trouble. "Someone else shot the gun," he said. Then, after officers told him that other kids had seen him firing the weapon, he changed his tune. He said that he'd brought the gun to school to scare people "like on television" and had shot Kayla because she had angered him by slapping his hand.

But despite that admission of guilt, Dedrick Owens was never going to be charged with any offense. A U.S. Supreme Court statute dating back to 1893 stipulates that no one under the age of seven years can be found guilty of a felony. If anyone was going to take the fall, it was going to be the person who had left a loaded firearm within easy reach of a child.

That person turned out to be 19-year-old Jamelle James, who lived with Dedrick's uncle at the crack house and owned the murder weapon. James would eventually plead no contest to involuntary manslaughter and would spend two years behind bars before being released. No one else has ever been brought to book for the senseless killing of Kayla Rolland.

Dedrick Owens and his brother were given up by their mother in the aftermath of the shooting and were placed in foster care. The Buell Elementary School closed its doors in 2002 due to a sharp fall in enrollments. The building was demolished in 2009.

Marlene Olive & Chuck Riley

Jim and Naomi Olive were a golden couple, she a one-time beauty queen, he a senior executive in the oil industry who was tipped for the very top. The couple lived an opulent lifestyle in Norfolk, Virginia, but if there was one thing missing from their lives it was a child. After receiving the devastating news that Naomi was unable to conceive, they decided to adopt. In 1959, they brought home a newborn baby girl who'd been given up at birth by her unwed mother. They named her Marlene, and it wasn't long before she was the center of their universe.

In 1962, Jim Olive accepted a job with Gulf Oil and moved his family to Guayaquil, Ecuador. Here, the Olives enjoyed an even grander lifestyle, with a large villa and an army of servants. Marlene had grown to be a delightful toddler who had developed a close bond with her adoptive father. Her relationship with Naomi, though, was less congenial. Left alone for long periods of time due

to her husband's demanding work hours, Naomi Olive had taken to
the bottle and was already showing the first signs of the mental
illness that would plague her for the rest of her life. When she was
drunk (which was often), she'd take out her frustrations on her
daughter, screaming at her and taunting her about her real
mother, who Naomi claimed had been a prostitute. This abuse
continued as Marlene aged and eventually started arguing back. As
the relationship became increasingly fractious, mother and
daughter were often at each other's throats, with Jim having to
step in and separate them.

Then, in 1973, Jim lost his job with Gulf Oil and announced to his
family that they were moving back to the United States. To
Marlene, now 13, it was a disaster. She'd spent most of her life in
Ecuador and loved it there. She desperately wanted to stay.
Everything she'd heard about the lifestyles of teens in the United
States was negative. She was particularly concerned about the
drug culture, fearful that she'd be sucked into it. She said as much
to her father. He laughed it off. Marlene was a good girl who did
well in school. He had no reason to believe that it would be any
different after they returned home.

And so, in 1973, Jim Olive moved his family to affluent Marin
County, California. He no longer had a fat corporate salary to rely
on, but to a go-getter like Jim, that was a minor, and temporary,
problem. He quickly acquired a partner and set up a business that
offered consulting services. That, of course, took up a serious
chunk of his time. Perhaps that is why he appears to have been

blissfully unaware of the deepening resentment between Naomi and Marlene.

That resentment had now progressed to a point of no return with taunts and insults openly traded and altercations sometimes becoming physical. As a result, Marlene began spending more and more time away from the home. Inevitably, she fell in with a bad crowd, a group of teenaged girls known for their drug-taking and promiscuity. Soon the 14-year-old was experimenting with marijuana, cocaine, and LSD, engaging in sex and skipping school to travel to rock concerts. She also developed an interest in the occult and would boast to friends that she was a member of the Church of Satan. That wasn't the only story she made up. She boasted that she had appeared in a child porn movie while living in South America, and said that her father was an important man in the Ecuadorian drug trade. And her mode of dress had changed, too. She dressed, quite frankly, like a streetwalker, her platform shoes and ultra-short skirts augmented by multi-colored hair and tons of make-up. At school, she gained a reputation for being "easy." The fears she'd expressed to her father about leaving Ecuador appeared to have been a self-fulfilling prophecy.

Many kids, of course, rebel during their teens, and some even go as far off the rails as Marlene Olive before self-correcting as they gain maturity. Marlene, an intelligent girl, might well have come to a similar realization as she matured. But in October 1974, an event occurred that would spin Marlene's life off in an entirely different direction. That was the month that she met 19-year-old Chuck Riley.

Chuck was your typical teenaged loser, a pudgy high school dropout, who'd never had a girlfriend and was, in fact, still a virgin when he met Marlene. No one in her circle would have paid him the slightest bit of attention except for one thing. Chuck was a drug dealer who drew his clientele mainly from the local teens. That was how he met Marlene and, after that first meeting, came to the conclusion that he was madly in love with her.

Marlene, at first, spurned Chuck's clumsy advances. He was overweight and awkward and despite having some street cred as a dealer, he was considered a joke by most of the "cool" kids that she hung out with. But eventually, after several months, his persistence wore her down, and she agreed to go out with him. Maybe it was the free drugs he gave her, or perhaps it was the expensive gifts he showered her with.

Whatever the case, Marlene must soon have realized that Chuck was a blank canvas, someone that she could manipulate to her will. Shortly after she allowed him to have sex with her, the 15-year-old Marlene began pushing the sexually naïve Chuck to more and more extreme limits. Once she ordered him to take explicit photos of her which she said she was going to send to Penthouse magazine; then she made him don a leather mask and other S&M gear and whip her; on another occasion, she masturbated herself with a loaded .22 pistol that he owned; taking things even further, she once urinated on his face while several of her friends stood watching. If Chuck ever wavered, she reminded him that she'd cast a witchcraft spell on him which made him her slave. Apparently, he believed her.

Chuck's relationship with Marlene had a distinct impact on his personality. Whereas before he'd been a jovial loser, eager to please and the butt of all jokes, he now was more assertive, less cordial, not as accommodating. He lost weight and began dressing more fashionably, he started carrying a gun. To Marlene's parents, though, he was just the kind of positive influence she needed in her life. Around them, he was always polite and respectful. Jim and Naomi happily gave their blessing to the relationship. Little did they know that their daughter had already begun nagging her boyfriend to murder them.

By now, Marlene's relationship with Naomi had devolved into all-out warfare. And the close bond she'd once enjoyed with Jim had also deteriorated. She blamed him for not backing her up in her fights with Naomi. Things finally came to a head in March 1975, when Chuck and Marlene were arrested for shoplifting. No charges were brought, but Jim Olive had finally had enough. He told Marlene that he was going to send her away to school and forbade her from seeing Chuck again. She, of course, disobeyed him and continued meeting with Chuck in secret. During those meetings, she told him that he was going to lose her if he did not do something soon. She encouraged him to find a hitman to get rid of her parents, adding that he could take over Jim's supposed South American drug empire once he was gone. She also issued her usual threats. If Chuck did not get rid of her parents, she was going to break up with him.

Chuck Riley was placed in an impossible position. He loved Marlene with all his heart and could not imagine his life without her. He'd once attempted suicide when she'd told him that she was ending her relationship with him. Now, he stood to lose her again. On Saturday, June 21, 1975, he decided to act.

Chuck had been doing acid for several days, and on the day in question, he was so spaced out that he was barely able to walk. Several people saw him that morning, shuffling through the affluent Terra Linda neighborhood on his way to the Olive residence. What they would not have seen was the gun tucked into his waistband under his shirt.

Marlene and her father were not at home when Chuck arrived, so he entered through an unlocked door and headed for an upstairs bedroom where Naomi lay asleep in a drunken stupor. On route, Chuck had picked up a hammer that he found on a sideboard, and now he lifted it, held it above his head for a brief moment, and then brought it down with all his might.

The blow was delivered with such force that the hammerhead actually penetrated Naomi's skull and became lodged in her brain cavity. Chuck had to press down with his hand on her head, in order to wriggle it free. Then he raised it again and brought it down, then again. And still, Naomi wasn't dead. She lay on the bed with her skull a bloody mess of bone shards, blood and brain matter. An odd gurgling sound issued from her throat. It was then that Chuck heard the sound of a vehicle drawing to a stop outside. Jim and Marlene were back.

Chuck had to think fast and in his brain-addled condition, he decided that his best bet was to confront Jim Olive as he entered the house. He rushed downstairs and hid behind a couch, drawing his pistol as he did. But Jim spotted the bulky assassin as soon as he entered the room and demanded that he show himself. Chuck then stood up, his face and clothes spattered with blood and brain matter.

"What have you done?" Jim demanded, then perhaps realizing the answer to his own question, "I'll kill you!" He lunged for Chuck and Chucked raised the pistol and fired four times, killing Jim Olive on the spot.

Chuck and Marlene spent the rest of the day cleaning up the crime scene. After nightfall, they loaded the bodies into the family station wagon and drove to China Camp State Park, where they incinerated them in a barbecue pit. The following morning, someone called out the fire service and a lone fireman was dispatched to extinguish the remaining embers. The firefighter noticed bones among the ashes, but took them to be from a deer.

Over the following week, the teenaged killers lived together in the death house. They were hardly discreet about their actions, going on a spending spree with Jim Olive's credit cards, inviting friends around to do drugs, and attending a rock concert by the band, Yes. During that concert, Marlene suddenly started chanting: "I killed my parents! I killed my parents!" over and over again, getting progressively louder and louder. But hardly anyone could hear her over the sound of the band, and those who did took her admission as a joke.

The disappearance of the Olives, however, could not remain a secret forever. After trying for several days to contact Jim, his business partner eventually reported him missing to the police. A patrol car was dispatched to make inquiries. Dissatisfied with the answers provided by Marlene, the officers asked her to accompany them to the station.

Marlene told several different stories under interrogation. First, she said that her parents had gone to Lake Tahoe for a break. Then, she said that Jim had killed Naomi and fled. Then it was Naomi who was the killer. Finally, she admitted to the murders, implicating Chuck. He was arrested that same day and quickly cracked under interrogation, confessing to the murders but insisting that Marlene had cast a spell on him and made him do it.

Both Chuck and Marlene were charged with the so-called "Barbecue Murders," but as a juvenile, she was never going to do hard time. The sentence, when it came, was a mere two years in juvenile hall. Chuck, meanwhile, had been tried, found guilty, and sentenced to death. That sentence was later commuted to life in prison. Chuck, now in his fifties, remains incarcerated to this day.

As for Marlene, she served part of her sentence at the Ventura School before being released to live under supervised care. While on parole, she fled to New York City where she worked for a time as a prostitute before being arrested and sent back to California to finish her sentence. She was released in 1980, at the age of 21.

Since then, Marlene Olive has been in and out of trouble with the law, serving several prison terms for forgery and drug-related charges. She and Chuck only saw each other once more, when she visited him in prison in 1981.

Joshua Phillips

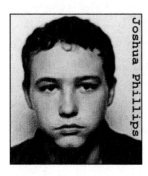

Joshua Earl Patrick Phillips was born on March 17, 1984, in Jacksonville, Florida. He was raised in a strict home and grew to be a personable and happy young man, a mediocre student at Philip Randolph Academies of Technology, but a boy who was nonetheless popular with his classmates and considered somewhat of a joker. Like most young boys, he loved sports and was particularly fond of baseball, which he often played with other kids on his block.

Not all of Joshua's playmates, though, were boys or even in his age group. One of his regular baseball partners was eight-year-old Maddie Clifton, whose family lived across the street from the Phillips family. Maddie was a happy and outgoing child, a bit of a tomboy who was the star of her school basketball team but, like Josh, had a fondness for baseball. The two of them were often seen together, one pitching and the other swinging. Josh's father, in fact, had warned him to stay away from Maddie, saying that the girl was too young to be his playmate. And Josh had complied. His father, Steve, had a temper. Josh did not want to cross him.

On the afternoon of November 3, 1998, however, temptation was thrown into Joshua's path. He'd been up in his bedroom playing on his computer when there was a knock at the door. It was Maddie and she wanted to play. Josh initially said no, citing his father's warnings and the fact that he still had chores to do. But Maggie was insistent, and eventually she wore him down. "Okay," he agreed. "We can toss a few pitches in the yard, but then you'll have to go." That was at around 5 p.m.

At 6:30 p.m., Maddie's mother, Sheila, called Maddie and her older sister Jessie in for dinner. Jessie responded almost right away but said that she didn't know where her sister was. Mother and daughter then carried out a quick and increasingly frantic search of the neighborhood. Unable to find Maddie, Sheila then ran back to the house and dialed 911. By the time her husband Steve arrived home from work minutes later, units had already been dispatched. Soon a torchlight search was underway, involving police officers and just about everyone in the neighborhood. It would endure throughout the night but without success. Maddie Clifton appeared to have vanished off the face of the earth.

Over the days that followed, the search continued around the clock while the police started fanning out through the neighborhood, going door to door and asking questions. Had anyone seen the little girl? Had they picked up on anything unusual? Had they noticed any strangers in the neighborhood? Nobody had. Even Joshua Phillips (who had decidedly seen Maddie on the day she disappeared) remained silent.

Then, on the morning of November 10, the mystery of the missing girl was resolved in a way that no one could have foreseen. Josh Phillips had departed for school as usual that day, kissing his mom goodbye before he left to catch the school bus. Missy Phillips then went about her household chores, which included tidying her son's bedroom. Josh had been somewhat reticent about her entering the room lately, but today she was going to have to do it. The space had an odd and unpleasant smell about it.

Entering the room, Missy thought that she saw the source of the problem. There was a small puddle at the foot of Josh's waterbed. Perhaps the spilled water was what was causing the stench. Missy grabbed one end of the mattress and peeled it back from the baseboard. Almost immediately she let it fall back into place and took a step back, bringing her hand up to her mouth as an involuntary gasp escaped her. Then she was turning and running, down the stairs and out into the street where she found a police officer. What Missy had seen crammed under the mattress was a human foot.

It did not take long before police cars were streaming through the quiet Jacksonville neighborhood, some with sirens wailing. Then there were officers stringing up crime scene tape around the

Phillips residence to hold back the crowd that had rapidly gathered. Among that crowd was Sheila Clifton, wondering what the ruckus was about and hoping against hope that it did not have anything to do with her daughter. The dreadful truth was confirmed when a police officer tracked her down and ushered her back home. Maddie's body had been found stashed under Joshua Phillips's bed.

While CSI units began working the scene, a patrol car was dispatched to Joshua's school with instructions to bring him to a local police station. There detectives began questioning the boy in the presence of his parents. It was pointless denying involvement in Maddie's death, and Phillips didn't try to. Instead, he concocted a story which the interrogators had difficulty believing.

According to Phillips, Maddie had arrived at his door begging him to play a game of baseball with her. He had eventually agreed, but they'd only been playing a short while when an accident occurred. He'd struck the ball particularly firmly and it had hit Maddie in the face, opening up a gash above her eye. Maddie had immediately fallen to the ground and started screaming.

Phillips had panicked. His father had warned him about playing with the little girl, and now he'd not only defied that order but had caused the child a serious injury. And his father would be home soon, meaning that he'd be in deep trouble. He therefore decided to pick Maddie up and carry her to his room, hoping that he could calm her down there.

But Maddie wasn't to be silenced. Lying on the floor of his bedroom, she again began wailing. His solution was to hit her twice on the head with his baseball bat and then to stab her in the throat with a pocket knife he was carrying. Then, believing she was dead, he pushed her under the mattress. He was just about to leave when Maddie started crying again so he pulled her out from under the bed and inflicted another knife wound to her throat. Then, as she lay still, he pushed her under the bed and left. Later he'd join in the search for the missing girl, knowing all the while that she was lying dead in his room.

Phillips had delivered his version of events with apparent sincerity, but the police already knew that he was lying. The ball that he claimed had hit Maddie in the eye had no traces of blood on it, and there was no blood in the yard where he claimed they'd been playing. The pathologist's report would also fill in the details of Maddie's injuries that Phillips had omitted. She had not been stabbed twice but nine times, and she'd been struck on the head hard enough to fracture her skull. The autopsy had also determined that she'd still been alive when Phillips had pushed her under the bed. The little girl had died in fear and pain.

Joshua Phillips was charged with first-degree murder and was tried as an adult. At his trial (held in Polk County due to massive media coverage of the case), his defense peddled the same story that he'd earlier told the police. But the prosecution was able to provide a far more feasible motive. They believed that this was a sex crime. Even though the autopsy did not reveal any sexual assault, Maddie's body was found nude from the waist down. The police were also able to determine that Phillips had been viewing violent pornographic images online just before the murder which they believed might had incited him to kill. Maddie's sister, Jessica, had already testified that Phillips had spoken to her and Maddie about sex in the past.

In the end, it took the jury just two hours to find Joshua Phillips guilty as charged. The judge then handed down the mandatory sentence of life in prison without the possibility of parole. The sentence was upheld on appeal in 2002.

Joshua Phillips is currently incarcerated at the Cross City Correctional Institution in Dixie County, Florida. In 2012, he was handed some hope of one day being released when the U.S. Supreme Court ruled that sentencing juveniles to life without parole is unconstitutional. A new sentencing hearing is pending at this time.

Evan Ramsey

On a summer morning in 1986, a man named Don Ramsey walked into the offices of the Anchorage Times in Anchorage, Alaska. Ramsey was heavily armed, with an AR 223 semi-automatic assault rifle, a snub-nosed .44 Magnum revolver, and over 200 rounds of ammunition. He was intent on carnage. The editor of this rag had refused to publish a political letter he'd written. Ramsey was going to make him pay for his lack of respect.

But Ramsey did not gain the retribution he was after that morning. In fact, he fired neither of his weapons. Instead, he took some hostages, shouted some abuse and eventually surrendered after a standoff with police. The offense, however, was serious enough to earn him a ten-year prison sentence. The authorities do not take kindly to private citizens brandishing weapons and making threats of violence.

And so, Don Ramsey's moment of madness landed him behind bars. His sentence, however, would not be suffered alone. It would have a profound effect on those closest to him, his wife and three young sons. Already a heavy drinker, Mrs. Ramsey lapsed into alcoholism under the pressure of raising three boys alone. Then, after the family home burned down, the Anchorage Department of Youth and Family Services stepped in to the remove the boys from their mother's custody. Ten-year-old John would be placed with one family; 7-year-old Evan and five-year-old William with another. Between 1988 and 1991, Evan and William would live in eleven different foster homes.

It was hardly a stable environment for the youngsters to grow up in. At several of their placements, the boys suffered physical and sexual abuse. Evan, who was a bit slow, got the worst of it. William would later recall how one pair of foster parents would pay the other children in the house to attack him as part of a sick game. Driven to despair by the constant mistreatment, 10-year-old Evan attempted suicide.

Then, in 1991, there was finally some respite for the brothers when a family named Hare adopted them. Their adoptive mother, Sue, was superintendent of the school district in Bethel, southwestern Alaska. It was several steps up from the foster homes where they'd been living.

Bethel is an isolated place. With a population of just 5,471 residents, it cannot be reached by road and is in an area so remote that locals called it simply "the bush." There is only one (junior) school, and Evan and his brother were enrolled there. The next couple of years were probably the happiest of their young lives.

But all of that was to change when Evan graduated to Bethel Regional High School. There he quickly became a target for bullies who homed in on his learning disabilities and called him "retard" or "spaz." He was also given the nickname "Screech," after a nerdy character in the sitcom Saved by the Bell.

Evan was not without friends, though. Among the 450 kids at his school, he was particularly close to 14-year-olds James Randall and Matthew Charles. The trio would often hang out after school, when they'd spend hours at the computer game Doom, a role-playing challenge in which the characters stalk and kill each other. (Doom was also a favorite of Columbine shooters, Eric Harris and Dylan Klebold). When not engaged in the game, Evan and his cohorts would draw up lists of students and teachers they'd like to kill. Top of Evan's list were a couple of ninth-graders, a boy and a girl, who constantly tormented him, calling him stupid and spitting in his hair.

How did it go from here, from computer games and fantasy hit lists, to an actual school shooting? We may never know. Suffice to say that when Evan first floated the idea, he received enthusiastic backing from his two friends. Matthew Charles spoke rapturously about the infamy he'd garner from his act while James Randall provided more tangible support. He began teaching Evan how to load and fire a twelve-gauge, pump-action shotgun. All that was needed now was a catalyst. It came after Evan's adoptive mother told him that his father had been released from prison.

On the morning of Wednesday, February 19, 1997, Evan Ramsey stepped off the school bus at Bethel Regional High. He was wearing a pair of baggy pants which allowed him to conceal on his person a Mossberg 12-gauge shotgun, provided to him by his friend James Randall. Ramsey walked directly to the commons area, where over a hundred students were gathered. He immediately brandished the shotgun, firing at the boy closest to him, hitting 15-year-old Josh Palacios in the abdomen. As Palacios collapsed to the floor, bleeding from a fatal stomach wound, a scream went up. Then the entire mass of students was in motion, fleeing like a herd of antelope before a large predator. Ramsey fired again, then again, each blast finding its target but not delivering a fatal shot.

Then an extraordinary thing happened. Even as the students were fleeing in panic, Ramsey saw somebody walking towards him. It was art teacher, Reyne Athanas, who had heard the gunshots and had rushed to the commons to find their source. Despite the obvious danger to her own life, the teacher tried to convince Ramsey to lay down his weapon. It is a miracle she wasn't shot.

Ramsey, however, was not about to surrender just yet. He had two specific targets in mind, the two ninth-graders who were his nemesis. ("I hated them as much as Hitler hated the Jews," he'd later confess.) Ramsey entered the main lobby, walking in the direction that most of the students had fled. The Mossberg was held across his waist, barrel pointing towards the ground but ready to be brought into a firing position in an instant. When school principal Ron Edwards stepped into his path, Ramsey did not even think. He lifted the shotgun and fired, pumped and fired again. Then, even as Edwards collapsed to the floor, Ramsey turned and walked back into the commons. He sat down on the floor and placed the gun barrel under his chin. That was how the police found him when they arrived moments later. Confronted by the officers, Ramsey said simply: "I don't want to die." Then he laid down his weapon and surrendered.

Evan Ramsey was taken into custody. In the meantime, an astonishing detail had emerged about the shooting. It appeared that as many as twenty students had known in advance that it was coming. Many of these individuals had stood on the library balcony overlooking the commons and watched the carnage below. Some had even taken photographs. And yet, not one of these kids had informed the authorities or a parent, a move that would have averted the tragedy.

As it was, two people were dead. Josh Palacios had been a popular student and a star athlete; Principal Edwards had been a U.S. Marine before taking up a teaching career. Several other kids had been injured in the carnage. Ramsey was going to have to pay for that.

On December 2, 1998, 16-year-old Evan Ramsey was found guilty of two counts of first-degree murder, three counts of first-degree attempted murder, and fifteen counts of third-degree assault. He was sentenced to 210 years in prison, which was reduced to two 99-year terms on appeal. Still, Ramsey will be 85 years old before he comes up for parole. He is currently incarcerated at the Spring Creek Correctional Center in Seward, Alaska.

Austin Sigg

The signs were there for all to see, clues that all was not right and that trouble lay ahead. But such indicators can be subtle and difficult to interpret. How is one to distinguish between the shy, introverted teen and the budding psychopath, head filled with visions of wanton slaughter? One clue might have been the violent child pornography found on Austin Sigg's computer when he was just thirteen years old. That particular indiscretion had earned Sigg a couple of sessions with a psychologist, who had beseeched the boy's father to restrict his son's internet access. Whether that advice was ever heeded is uncertain.

Fast-forward four years to 2012 and we find Austin Sigg enrolled in the forensic science program at Arapahoe Community College in Littleton, Colorado. The obviously intelligent teen had quit school the previous year, driven out by bullies who constantly picked on him because of his high-pitched voice. A high school equivalency test had seen him admitted to college, but even here he remained isolated from his classmates. They found him "weird," "frighteningly intense" and "obsessed with death." While most of the forensics students hoped for a career in law enforcement, Austin informed them that he planned on becoming a mortician.

But perhaps there was another reason for Austin Sigg's choice of major; perhaps he thought that a knowledge of police detection techniques would be useful to him in the secondary vocation he was planning. Austin, you see, had never outgrown his childhood fascination with sexual violence. Like most budding psychopaths, he'd spent years nurturing the violent images that circulated in his brain. In his case, those visions centered not on aberrant sex or the act of murder. His particular fetish was for dissection. The thought of having a human body to carve apart and examine instilled in him a feeling of sexual arousal that was almost too intense to bear. Eventually, it drove him to action.

On the morning of Monday, May 28, 2012, Sigg got into his Jeep Cherokee and drove to Ketner Lake, near his home in Westminster, Colorado. Concealed within his pocket was a bottle of chloroform which he'd cooked up using a recipe he'd found on the internet. His plan was cursory at best. He was going to conceal himself in bushes beside some isolated path and wait for a lone female to pass by. He'd then come up behind her and clamp a chloroform-soaked rag over her face. After she passed out, he'd drag her into the bushes and rape her. He might even strangle her to death and then cut her. He hadn't decided on that part yet.

Sigg didn't have to wait long for a potential victim to appear. He'd barely crouched down in the brush when he spotted a female jogger coming up the path towards him. Steadying his nerves with a couple of deep breaths, he waited until she passed and then broke cover with his chloroform cloth in hand. The woman, however, must have heard him because she turned just as he was about to grab her. A brief struggle then ensued before the potential victim broke free and sprinted away. She later reported the incident to the police. By the time they arrived, Austin Sigg was long gone.

Sigg was frustrated but not discouraged by his failure. He realized now that he'd made a crucial mistake in targeting a victim who was strong enough to fight back. What he needed was someone who was easy to overpower. He'd always had a preference for children anyway.

Jessica Ridgeway was a joy to all who knew her. The fifth-grader was a bundle of energy with a mischievous sense of humor and a genuinely caring nature. She loved the color purple and performing in the peewee cheerleading squad at Witt Elementary. She was on her way to that school on October 5, 2012, when she disappeared.

At around 10 a.m. that morning, a school administrator placed a courtesy call to Jessica's mother, wanting to find out if Jessica was okay. Sarah Ridgeway, however, did not get the call as she was asleep, having just returned home from working a night shift. It was only at 4:30 p.m. that she picked up her voice mail and learned that her daughter was missing. She immediately called the Westminster police, but it would be five hours before all of the criteria was met to issue an Amber Alert.

By then, a massive search was already underway, one that would eventually involve over 1,000 police and civilian volunteers. But as the days passed with no sign of the missing girl, hopes of finding her alive began to appear more and more remote. And the optimism of investigators was not improved when Jessica's backpack was found on a sidewalk in Superior, over six miles from her home. That discovery seemed to indicate that Jessica had been abducted. The backpack did, however, provide the Colorado Bureau of Investigation with a piece of evidence that could be checked for trace DNA. They'd only just sent the bag off for processing when they got the news everyone had been dreading.

Late on the afternoon of October 11, two municipal workers discovered a heavy garbage bag near Pattridge Park Open Space in Arvada. One of the men split the bag open with his pocket knife and shook its contents out onto the ground. Moments later the two men reeled back in horror. The bag contained the dissected torso of a child.

Jessica Ridgeway had been found, but her killer was still out there, and a ripple of fear ran through the community. What kind of a monster would murder and mutilate an innocent little girl, and how long before he targeted another child? As concerned parents began escorting their children to and from class, officers guarded crosswalks and photographed cars parked outside schools. Meanwhile, Westminster took on a mantle of purple as residents adorned their mailboxes in ribbons to honor Jessica. At around that time, the police also issued a public appeal, urging citizens to come forward with any information, no matter how trivial. On October 19, one of them heeded the call.

The caller did not have anything tangible to share. All he would say was that the police should talk to Austin Sigg, a local teen who the informant insisted was "obsessed with death." On the face of it, that did not seem like a very promising lead, but the police were desperate for a break in the case, and so two CBI agents visited Sigg's residence that same afternoon. The youngster was entirely co-operative, answering questions and agreeing to provide DNA for testing. By the time the agents left with DNA samples in hand, they were convinced that they'd been sent on a fool's errand.

But the case was about to take a dramatic turn. On October 23, before the results of Sigg's DNA test were in, a 911 dispatcher in Jefferson County received a most unusual call. The caller identified herself as Mindy Sigg. This is the actual transcript.

Mindy Sigg: "Hi, um, I need you to come to my house … um, my son wants to turn himself in for the Jessica Ridgeway murder."

Dispatcher: "And what's going on there? Ma'am, are you there?"

Mindy Sigg: "Did you not hear me? He just confessed to killing her."

Dispatcher: "I know. I want you to tell me what's going on. Can you tell me exactly what he said?"

Mindy Sigg: "That he did it and gave me details and her remains are in my house."

The dispatcher then asked if she could speak to Austin directly.

Austin Sigg: "I don't exactly get why you're asking me these questions. I murdered Jessica Ridgeway."

Dispatcher: "Okay."

Austin Sigg: "There is ... I have proof that I did it ... there is no other question. You just have to send a squad car down here."

The squad car had, in fact, already been dispatched. When the officers arrived, Sigg was true to his word. He gave himself up without offering any resistance. As a juvenile, he was taken to the Mount View Services Center and it was there that detectives began interrogating him. He seemed almost keen to tell his story.

Asked why he'd chosen Jessica, Sigg simply shrugged and said that she was at the 'wrong place, wrong time.' "I was just driving and just kind of looking," he said. "And I saw her. And I parked, and I waited. And she walked by, and I grabbed her."

He said that he'd pulled her into the back seat of his car and had secured her arms and legs with zip ties. He'd then driven around for a while before taking her back to his house. There he told her to change into some clothes that he'd picked out for her. Then he put on a movie for her to watch while he cut her hair. Finally, he tried to strangle her, using a zip tie. When that cut into his hands and failed to provide the right amount of leverage, he resorted to manual strangulation, throttling her for about three minutes until she blacked out.

But Jessica was still not dead, and as she lay twitching on the floor, Sigg dragged her to the bathroom, filled the tub with scalding hot water and drowned her in it. He then began dissecting the corpse in the bath, neatly wrapping and labeling the body parts. Some of these he'd later discard. Others, like the head and vagina, he'd keep hidden in the crawlspace beneath the house.

Asked why he had dismembered the body, Sigg said that he was fulfilling a sexual fantasy. However, he emphatically denied sexually assaulting the ten-year-old. This, the medical examiner would determine, was a lie. Jessica had indeed been raped.

And so Austin Sigg was brought before the Jefferson County District Court in October 2013. Against the advice of counsel, he entered guilty pleas to all of the charges, secure in the knowledge that his age at the time of the murder precluded him from the death penalty.

In fact, the mandated sentence for someone of his age was life in prison, with parole eligibility after 40 years. Judge Stephen Munsinger, however, was determined that Sigg should spend the rest of his days behind bars. He sentenced Sigg to an additional 86 years to run consecutively with his life sentence. That means that if Sigg ever earns parole, he will immediately have to begin serving the 86-year term. It is unlikely that he will ever walk the streets again.

That, of course, is of scant consolation to Jessica Ridgeway's grieving family. A monster entered their lives in October 2012, cruelly snatching away a precious little girl for no other reason than to satisfy his perverted needs. To quote a line from Judge Munsinger's closing statement: "Evil is real. It was present in our community on October 5, 2012. On that day, its name was Austin Sigg."

Jasmine Richardson

Marc and Debra Richardson were none too keen on the man their daughter wanted to date. And who could blame them. Jasmine was, after all, just 12 years old, a mature twelve admittedly, who looked older than her years, but still essentially a child. The man she'd fallen for was 23, an unemployed high school dropout who liked dressing all in black and wearing eye makeup. Not only that but Jeremy Steinke claimed to be a 300-year-old werewolf and wore a vial of blood around his neck. It is easy to see why the Richardsons forbade their daughter from having anything to do with him.

But that ruling did not go down well with Jasmine, and despite her parents' warnings, she continued to see Steinke. Unbeknownst to Marc and Debra, Steinke had already asked Jasmine to marry him, and the pretty twelve-year-old had said yes.

How the young lovers planned to conclude their underage wedding is unknown, but it seems that at least part of the plan was to get rid of anyone who stood in the way of their relationship. They'd been pretty open about their intentions. Posting on the popular Canadian social media site, Nexopia, in March 2006, Jasmine had written: "I hate them. So I have this plan, it begins with me killing them and ends with me living with you." Steinke, posting under the name 'Soul Eater,' had responded: "Well, I love your plan, but we need to get a little more creative with like details and stuff."

On April 23, 2006, a neighbor of the Richardsons in Medicine Hat, Alberta, called the police to say that she was concerned about the family. According to the neighbor, her son had gone over to the Richardson house to play with the family's 8-year-old son, Jacob. Getting no response when he rang the doorbell, the youngster had peered through some windows and had spotted a "blood covered body." Then boy had then run home to tell his mother. She had been too scared to see for herself and had instead called the police.

A unit was immediately dispatched to the address to check it out, with the officers later admitting that they'd expected it to be a false alarm. It wasn't. Sprawled on the basement floor were the bodies of 42-year-old Marc Richardson and his wife Debra, 48. The couple had been viciously knifed to death, Debra suffering twelve stab wounds and Marc suffering twice as many, even as he tried to defend himself with a screwdriver. The killer had then dipped his hands in their blood and painted a series of bloody handprints on the walls. It was a savage killing, and it left the officers fearing the worst for the Richardsons' two children, 12-year-old Jasmine and 8-year-old, Jacob.

The whereabouts of the boy were quickly established, and it was bad. He was lying on the bed in his upstairs bedroom, his throat slashed from ear to ear and blackened blood staining the bedding. Of Jasmine, however, there was no trace.

Initially, the police feared that Jasmine had been the victim of an abduction. Perhaps she had been the object of the attack, and the killer had murdered the family in order to get to her. That speculation, however, was quickly dismissed when detectives spoke to Jasmine's friends and found out about Jeremy Steinke. Jasmine's boyfriend was said to be an immature young man with drink and drug problems, who boasted that he enjoyed the taste of blood. Then, after investigators were directed to the couple's Nexopia pages and read their posts, an all-points bulletin was issued for the fugitives. They were traced that very same day to the town of Leader, Saskatchewan, some 100 miles away.

Jeremy Steinke and Jasmine Richardson were questioned separately, and both initially denied involvement in the killings. But the evidence against them quickly started stacking up. They had hardly been discreet about their intentions. First there were those incitements to murder, posted on a public forum. Then there was the testimony of Jasmine's friends. They said that she spoke openly about killing her parents and that they had heard her asking Steinke directly to murder them. It was also learned that

Steinke had approached a number of his friends and asked for their help in carrying out the murders.

None of this, of course, amounted to evidence of murder. The police were still desperate to get a confession out of the killers, and to do it, they relied on one of the oldest tricks in the book. They placed an undercover cop in Jeremy Steinke's cell. It wasn't long before they had the admission they needed.

"You hear about that triple homicide?" Steinke said during a secretly recorded conversation. "Yeah, that was me. Me and my old lady have become legends." Speaking of the killings themselves, he told the officer that he'd drunk a six pack of beer and done some cocaine before entering the Richardson house that night. Of Marc Richardson's murder, he boasted: "I gutted him like a fish."

And then Steinke dropped a bombshell. Up until now, the police had believed that he had carried out the murders on his own and that Jasmine's role had been as an accessory before and after the fact. But what Steinke said next revealed a far more sinister truth. "She cut her little brother's throat and it didn't bother her at all. She didn't cry or anything. In fact, the next day when we were on the road, she was laughing about it. She's got a few screws loose, that girl." Steinke also told the undercover officer Marc Richardson's final word was, "Why?"

"Because your daughter wanted it that way," had been his reply.

Both Jeremy Steinke and Jasmine Richardson were charged with three counts of first-degree murder. In his case, the court proceedings were relatively simple. Found guilty on all counts, he received the maximum allowable under Canadian law – life in prison with parole eligibility in 25 years.

Jasmine Richardson's trial presented prosecutors with far more restrictive legal conditions. Under Canada's Youth Criminal Justice Act, she could not be tried as an adult and could not receive a sentence longer than ten years. On July 9, 2007, she was found guilty of three counts of first-degree murder, and in November 2007, she received the maximum penalty.

As Jasmine had already been behind bars for eighteen months awaiting trial, it meant that she'd only serve another eight-and-a-half years. And none of that time would be spent in an actual prison. For the first four years, she would receive treatment in a psychiatric institution. Thereafter, she would serve four-and-a-half years under conditional supervision in the community.

Jasmine Richardson was released from custody in 2016 and has since graduated with a degree from the University of Calgary. Jeremy Steinke remains behind bars.

Nathaniel Abraham

Nathaniel Abraham was eleven years old and he had a gun, an ancient, poorly-maintained gun admittedly, one that was missing its stock, but a gun nonetheless, a weapon more than capable of dispensing death. No one knows exactly how the sixth-grader had come upon the .22 rifle, but there was little doubt about what he planned to do with it. He'd been practicing for days, he told his classmates, going out into the woods and firing at balloons. One of these days, he bragged, he was going to shoot someone.

These may have sounded like idle boasts coming from an eleven-year-old, but Nate Abraham was far from your ordinary pre-teen. He was a kid with issues: anger issues, learning issues, issues with the law. Over the prior two years, he'd been picked up twenty-two times by the police, and some of the charges had related to weapons offences. Now, on the evening of Oct. 29, 1997, he picked up his rifle and went looking for a victim.

The first person who Nathaniel drew a bead on that fateful night
was his neighbor, Michael Hudack. However, that bullet missed,
and Nathaniel ran off before Hudack even realized he'd been shot
at. Then he lay low for several hours building up his courage.
Eventually, he climbed a steep embankment near his home in
Pontiac, Michigan, and sat there under the stars surveying his
surroundings. The most prominent feature of the urban landscape
was a convenience store with its surrounding parking lot about
200 yards from where Nate now sat. Nate raised the rifle and
sighted along it, picking out various people as they arrived and
departed the store.

Eighteen-year-old Ronnie Greene was also out on that Friday
night, just chilling and hanging around, planning to meet up with
some friends later on. First, though, he had to drop by the
convenience store to pick up some supplies for the weekend.
Greene didn't know Nate Abraham, and he had no idea that the
rifle was tracking him as he exited the store and crossed the lot. Up
on the embankment, meanwhile, Nate was still sighting along the
barrel, his finger resting on the trigger guard as he tracked Greene.
His breathing was shallow, his chest constricted, barely rising. This
was it, he decided. This was the one. Slowly, his finger crept
towards the trigger and began applying gentle pressure to it. Then
the rifle kicked slightly in his hands and emitted its hollow snap.
Down in the parking lot, Ronnie Greene crumbled to the ground.

Nate Abraham didn't stick around to witness the carnage he'd
wrought. The minute he saw Greene fall, he was up and running,

back to his home where he hid the murder weapon. Down in the lot, meanwhile, onlookers had seen Greene collapse and had come to his aid. More than one of them had punched 911 into a phone, and soon came the wail of sirens and the sweep of police lights. An ambulance forced its way through the crowd, and paramedics scrambled to assist the wounded man. But it was too late. The bullet had entered high on the skull and had penetrated the brain. Ronnie Greene was likely dead before he even hit the ground.

Nathaniel Abraham might well have gotten away with the shooting of an innocent man. After all, the victim was a complete stranger to him and he'd fired from a sniping position. No one had seen him pull the trigger. But Nate could not keep quiet about the shooting. Why would he? He was proud of what he'd done. Over the following days at school, he boasted to classmates: "I done shot that nigger." It didn't take long before those boasts reached the ears of the faculty. From there, they were reported to the police. Within days of Ronnie Greene's death, his killer was in custody.

The case might well have landed Michigan prosecutors with a political landmine. After all, trying an eleven-year-old for murder is bound to illicit a public response. Already there were allegations in some quarters of a racist agenda. Fortunately, however, the state was able to fall back on a recently passed piece of legislation, the controversial Juvenile Waiver Law. This made it mandatory for juveniles to be tried as adults under certain conditions, and the Abraham case ticked all the boxes.

Thus it was that eleven-year-old Nathaniel Abraham became the youngest first-degree murder defendant in US history. By the time the matter eventually came to trial, Abraham was two years older but still very much a child, his feet barely reaching the floor as he sat at the defense table. That, according to counsel Geoffrey Fieger, was an abomination. Fieger denounced the Juvenile Waiver Law as barbaric and insisted that his client should never have faced an adult trial. Then he set about building a more practical defense. He contended that Abraham had never intended to kill and that he had been aiming at some trees when he'd shot Ronnie Greene. The rifle, he said, was in such poor shape that it could not be properly aimed and the shooting could not, therefore, have been deliberate. He also asserted that his client was mentally deficient, with the mental capacity of a six-year-old.

The prosecution, of course, had anticipated these arguments and countered them with some valid points of their own. These included Abraham's boasts before and after the murder, evidence that he'd practiced target shooting, and his attempt to gun down Michael Hudack on the same night that he killed Ronnie Greene.

In the end, it was the state's case that won out, although the jury did not deliver the first-degree verdict that prosecutors had hoped for. They found Nathaniel Abraham guilty of second-degree murder. Judge Eugene Moore then decided that, despite this being an adult trial, Abraham should be sentenced as a juvenile. He ordered that the young killer be detained at a juvenile facility until his twenty-first birthday, whereupon he would be set free.

Nathaniel Abraham did well behind bars, give or take the odd anger outburst, the odd theft, and an ingrained dislike for authority figures. While incarcerated, he completed his high school diploma and even gained entry to Wayne State University, where he hoped to train as a gym teacher after his release. That release came in January 2007 and was immediately engulfed in controversy when it was learned that the state had provided Abraham with a rent-free apartment and was paying for his college tuition. The dust had barely settled on those revelations when Abraham dropped out of Wayne State and announced that he was to pursue a career as a rapper. It was a quest for stardom that would ultimately fail.

Abraham, however, would not stay out of the headlines for long. In 2012, he was arrested at a Bay City service station and found to be in possession of 254 ecstasy pills. Charged with intent to distribute a controlled substance, he then compounded matters by assaulting two prison officials. He currently remains behind bars at Michigan State prison.

Seisaku Nakamura

Seisaku Nakamura was born in Hamamatsu, on Japan's central-west coast, in 1924. His early life was difficult. Seisaku was born deaf into a society that was less than sympathetic to such physical imperfections. Considered an embarrassment by his family because of his disability, he was frequently beaten, treated as an outcast and excluded from familial activities.

Perhaps unsurprisingly, this cruel treatment had a profound impact on the boy's psyche. Trapped within his silent world, Seisaku began to dream up elaborate fantasies in which he was a Samurai warrior exacting revenge against the residents of a village who had wronged him. He supplemented these fantasies by watching movies in which Samurai warriors slaughtered their victims with their lethal Katana swords. And he developed a near obsession with the warrior code and the need to defend one's honor.

And yet, on the surface, all appeared normal. Despite the roadblocks that genetics had placed in his path, Seisaku grew to be a bright boy, who enjoyed his studies and excelled at them. He'd also grown into a tall and strapping youth who, even in his teens, towered over his mother and father. Had he wanted, he could easily have snatched away the rod they enjoyed beating him with and turned it on them. Yet he remained polite and deferential towards his parents, enduring his many torments without complaint. Japanese children instinctively defer to older family members. When Nakamura struck out, it would be against strangers.

The first murders committed by Seisaku Nakamura occurred on August 22, 1938, when he was just 14 years of age. The victims were two young women who had offered resistance when he'd tried to rape them. The women's brutalized corpses were found soon after, both of them stabbed and slashed to death in what looked like a frenzied attack. The murders, however, were never made public. Japan was on a war footing at the time, preparing for its conquest of the Pacific. The authorities did not want to sully the patriotic fervor with front page news of a brutal double homicide. The crimes thus went unreported and uninvestigated. Nakamura had committed his first murders and had gotten away with them.

The teen killer's next foray into sexual homicide, however, was more difficult to ignore. It began on August 18, 1941, when a woman was found savagely stabbed to death and another was discovered alive but severely injured. The police were still trying to get to grips with those grisly crimes when three more victims were found stabbed and hacked to death.

Five women had now been attacked within the span of just three days, and yet the authorities again decided to withhold the details from the public. Senior military officers were afraid that the news might cause panic among a populace already feeling the strains of war. In the end, however, it was decided to launch an inquiry, even if it was just to placate the families of the murdered women.

And the investigation soon unearthed its first clue. A tall, well-built young man had been spotted walking casually away from at least two of the murder scenes. Might this be the killer? The police thought so and yet put very little effort into finding him. As a result, Nakamura avoided capture. And he was about to kill again.

On September 27, Nakamura was at his parental home when he got into an argument with his brother. Matters quickly got heated and then turned violent, with Nakamura drawing a knife and plunging it into his sibling's chest, killing him on the spot. He then turned the weapon on his terrified family, slashing and stabbing as they scurried for cover. Nakamura's father and sister, his sister-in-law and young niece, were all injured. Miraculously, all of them survived their wounds. Questioned about the incident, the family refused to name their attacker. They were too afraid of retribution, they said.

Sadly, that refusal would have tragic consequences for another family. On August 30, 1942, Nakamura spotted a young woman on the street and followed her home. Entering the residence, he dragged the woman to the ground and began ripping at her clothes. When the woman's husband tried to intercede, Nakamura drew a knife and slaughtered both him and his wife before turning his weapon on their terrified children. The younger boy and girl were stabbed and slashed to death before Nakamura homed in on the older girl. Grabbing her by the hair, he ripped at her clothes before throwing her naked to the floor. Then he straddled her, working at his belt buckle as the terrified girl squirmed beneath him. She fully expected to be raped and murdered, but then, inexplicably, Nakamura broke off the attack and fled.

The police, meanwhile, had been investigating the attack on the Nakamura family and had become convinced that the family was refusing to name their attacker because he was one of their own. Their suspicion was that 17-year-old Seisaku was responsible, but they had no way of proving it until the surviving victim of the latest atrocity provided them with a description of her attacker. It fit Seisaku Nakamura to a tee.

Nakamura offered no resistance when he was arrested on October 12, 1942. And he made no attempt to deny that he was the man responsible for the killing spree which now included nine known victims. He described his crimes with relish, even adding the two murders he'd committed as a 14-year-old, which the police had been unaware of. That brought his tally to eleven, and he was about to indirectly claim a twelfth victim. Weighed down by the guilt and shame of his son's murderous rampage, Nakamura's father, Fumisada, took his own life.

Criminal justice is usually delivered swiftly in Japan, and it was even more so during the war years. Just 17 years of age at the time, Nakamura was deemed an adult and was tried as such. A procession of doctors testified during the trial, each of them offering evidence that Nakamura was insane and should be confined to a mental hospital. The authorities, however, were determined to put the eleven-time killer to death. Found guilty on all charges, the 'Hamamatsu Deaf Killer' was sentenced to execution by hanging. That sentence was carried out on June 19, 1944.

Sam Manzie

When Sam Manzie was in the first grade, teachers at the Holy Family School in Lakewood, New Jersey, recommended that his parents send him for psychological evaluation. The boy, they said, had issues. He fought constantly with his classmates, was often sad, and would at other times sit with arms folded, fuming silently at the world around him and refusing to communicate. Those issues, according to the psychologist who examined him, were just adolescent growing pains.

And that evaluation appeared to be on the money as Sam progressed through grammar school. There were some disciplinary issues, sure, but in the main, the boy proved to have an above average intellect and consistently brought home good grades. By the time he entered Christian Brothers Academy as a ninth-grader in 1996, he had decided on a career path. Sam Manzie wanted to be a historian.

Still, Sam's path through the educational system had not been without its hiccups. He was an insular kid, with few friends and no interest in sports. His classmates called him "Manzie the Pansy." As a 13-year-old, he'd confided in his parents that he wanted to kill himself because "nobody understands me." After a long conversation on the issue, Sam's father, Nick, believed that he'd dissuaded his son from such foolish ideas. But Sam continued to lock himself in his room for hours on end, sitting at his computer. It was through this activity that he discovered the sordid world of gay chat rooms.

Toward the end of his freshman year, Sam was struck down by a mystery ailment that kept him away from classes for several weeks. When he tried to return, the school informed his parents that they would not accept him back unless he was committed for psychiatric treatment. What they didn't reveal to the Manzies was the reason for their stipulation. Sam had written a sexually explicit note to a male teacher.

The issue of Sam returning to school had by now turned into an irrelevance in any case. He informed his long-suffering parents that he had decided to drop out. Unbeknownst to the Manzies, their 14-year-old son had by now struck up an online friendship with a man named Steve Simmons, a 42-year-old convicted pedophile, who he'd met in the chat room he regularly frequented.

And that friendship soon progressed to more than just chat. In August 1996, Sam went to an arranged meeting with Simmons at the Raceway Mall in Freehold, New Jersey. Thereafter, they spent the night together at Simmons's home in Holbrook, Long Island.

Over the months that followed, Sam met Simmons regularly for sex at motels or at Simmons's home. The relationship only came to light after Nick Manzie noticed a Long Island number that appeared several times on his phone bill and decided to call it. Simmons admitted knowing Sam but said that they were just online buddies who had a mutual interest in computing. Mr. Manzie then warned Simmons to break off all contact with his son. Even so, he did not suspect a sexual relationship. Sam had once told his mother that he thought he might be gay, but his parents had refused to believe it.

By now, the bond between Sam and his parents had deteriorated to such a state that Nick Manzie once had to call 911 in response to one of the boy's rages. In the summer of 1997, they sent him to a psychiatrist who recommended admission to a structured program at the Shoreline Behavioral Health Center in Toms River. There, Sam was diagnosed with "major depression psychosis" and prescribed the anti-depressant drug, Paxil. He was also scheduled for a number of sessions with a psychiatrist, and it was during one of those sessions that he disclosed his relationship with Steve Simmons. Since Sam was still a juvenile, the doctor was required by law to inform the authorities, and he did so immediately.

The revelation of their teenaged son's gay relationship was devastating to the Manzies, who were strict Catholics. It sparked a whole new round of angry confrontations inside the family home. But Sam was at least prepared to cooperate with the police in gathering evidence against Simmons. He agreed to participate in a series of taped conversations, making two calls, on September 17 and September 19. A couple of days later, he had a change of heart, taking a hammer to the recording device. He also called Simmons and warned him that the police had him under surveillance.

The destruction of the surveillance equipment was the last straw for the Manzies. They decided that enough was enough and applied to have Sam committed to a residential psychiatric facility. Little did they know the problems they'd encounter in their attempts to do so. The family could not afford to keep Sam at Shoreline since their health insurance only covered the cost of treatment, not of residency. And having him committed to a state mental health facility also proved problematic. The matter eventually ended up in court, where a judge refused the application, instead urging the family to "go home and get along." This lack of appreciation for the depth of Sam Manzie's mental health issues would have tragic consequences.

On the afternoon of Saturday, September 27, 11-year-old Eddie Werner left his home in Jackson Township, New Jersey, and set off on a mission. Eddie was a happy and energetic little boy and he was applying those qualities to a fund-raising initiative at his school. He was going door to door selling candy and wrapping paper. The prize for the student who raised the most money was a pair of walkie-talkies, and Eddie was determined to win.

At around 5:30 that afternoon, Eddie Werner knocked on the Manzies' front door. Sam, who was home alone, opened it and then listened to the cheerfully delivered sales pitch. "Sure," he said, after Eddie had said his piece. "I'll buy some of your candy. Come on in."

Trustingly, Eddie entered the house and then followed Sam, as instructed, to an upstairs room. It was there that Manzie turned on the boy, first trying to force him into performing oral sex and then ordering him to strip. Eddie, 4' 8" and weighing just 70 pounds, was no match for the older boy. He was easily overpowered, sodomized and then strangled with the cord of an alarm clock. Manzie then stuffed the child's tiny corpse into a suitcase which he hid in his room. After nightfall, while his family was asleep, he crept out and hauled the case to a nearby wood, where he hid it in the undergrowth.

A search was launched that night, a search that would endure for two days before its denouement with the discovery of Eddie Werner's pitiful remains. By then, the story of the boy's disappearance was all over the news, and Dolores Manzie was living in dread that her son might somehow have been involved. Eventually, on October 1, she plucked up the courage to ask him directly. When Sam admitted that it was he who had strangled the little boy, his mother immediately called the police.

Sam Manzie was brought to trial for the murder of Eddie Werner in April 1999. Despite obvious issues surrounding his mental health, he pleaded guilty and was sentenced to 70 years behind bars. In another trial, Manzie's middle-aged lover, Steve Simmons, was convicted on child molestation charges and was sentenced to five years in prison.

Jesse Pomeroy

Jesse Pomeroy was born in Boston in 1859, the second son of Charles and Ruth Pomeroy. He was an awkward-looking child, big and hulking with a milky right eye and facial features that seemed too large, even for his over-sized head. He had an overly wide mouth, thin lips and large protruding ears. If that were not enough, he also suffered epileptic-like shaking episodes.

But, bizarre though his appearance was, it paled when compared to his abhorrent psychology. Pomeroy was a psychopath and a serial killer, a sexual sadist of immense brutality. True, he killed only two people, rather than the minimum of three prescribed in the FBI's definition, but he viciously tortured many others, and there is little doubt that he would have killed more had he not been caught. Given that he was only 14 at the time of his arrest, one shudders to think how many victims he might have slaughtered.

To understand how Pomeroy came to sexual sadism at so tender an age, you have to know something of his upbringing. Jesse's father, Charles Pomeroy, was a violent drunk who did not believe in sparing the rod on his children. Jesse and his siblings were punished for the slightest infraction, taken out behind the outhouse, stripped naked and beaten bloody, sometimes with a paddle, sometimes with a horsewhip. These beatings may have been intended to instill discipline, but they had an unwanted side effect on young Jesse. He began to derive sexual pleasure from pain and punishment. As he grew older, he began to find satisfaction in the suffering of others.

At first, he directed his violent outbursts against animals. The Pomeroy family dared not keep pets in the house because they invariably met with a violent end. Jesse once wrung the necks of a pair of lovebirds his mother kept. On another occasion, he was caught torturing a neighbor's kitten. But, as with most killers, he eventually tired of tormenting animals and turned his attention to human targets, specifically children smaller than himself.

His first known victim was William Paine. In December 1871, a couple of men climbing Powder Horn Hill, near Chelsea Creek in South Boston, heard a faint cry. It appeared to be coming from a small shack, so they went to investigate. Entering the building, the men were shocked to find a young boy, aged no more than four, suspended by his wrists from a rope tied to the wooden beams of the building. The boy was half-naked and semi-conscious, his lips turned blue by the cold, his hands purple due to the blood trapped by the rope. He'd obviously been severely beaten, and there were a number of ugly, red welts on his pale flesh.

The men cut the boy down and alerted the police. But young William was in no condition to identify his attacker and, with nothing to go on, the police were forced to abandon their inquiries. They just prayed that this was an isolated incident. It wasn't.

In February 1872, 7-year-old Tracy Hayden was lured to Powder Horn Hill on the pretense of "going to see the soldiers." Like William Paine, the diminutive boy was bound, beaten and tortured, his front teeth knocked out, his eyes blackened and his nose broken in a savage attack. He was then stripped naked and whipped, leaving deep welts on his back. Tracy told the police that his assailant had also threatened to cut off his penis. But he wasn't able to provide a description, other than to say that the teenaged boy who had attacked him had brown hair.

Just a couple of months later, Jesse Pomeroy struck again. After promising eight-year-old Robert Maier a trip to the circus, he lured the boy to his favorite lair. There he beat the youngster with a stick, forcing him to repeat obscenities while he was being assaulted. Robert later told police that Jesse fondled himself as he delivered the beating. He eventually freed the boy, threatening him with death if he told anyone.

By now, word of a pervert attacking young boys had leaked out, and the police were inundated with angry and fearful Boston parents. A massive manhunt was launched, during which police questioned hundreds of youths matching the vague description they had. All of their efforts came to nothing. Jesse Pomeroy evaded the dragnet.

He was at it again in mid-July 1872, luring an unsuspecting seven-year-old to the shack on Powder Horn Hill. The boy was stripped, bound, whipped and beaten. He was released with the threat of retribution if he told anyone what had happened.

In the wake of the latest attack, a $500 reward was offered for information leading to the arrest of the "inhuman scamp," as he was now dubbed by the press. The bounty brought vigilantes onto the streets, but even as they began patrolling, the attacks suddenly stopped.

Ruth Pomeroy, perhaps suspecting that her son might be responsible, decided to move her family across the river from Chelsea to the less affluent South Boston area. Not long after, the attacks started there.

George Pratt, a sickly seven-year-old, was treasure hunting along the South Boston shoreline when Pomeroy approached him and offered 25 cents for an errand. The boy agreed to accompany Pomeroy and ended up being overpowered and tied up. Pomeroy then launched his most violent attack yet, not only beating the boy, but tearing at his skin and biting a chunk of flesh from his cheek and another from his buttocks. He also stabbed George with a thick sewing needle and tried to stick the needle into his eye. The boy managed to avoid that injury by rolling onto his stomach, and Pomeroy then broke off the attack and fled.

This last assault saw a clear escalation to the violence wrought against his victims, and the next two attacks showed further evidence of Pomeroy's descent into degeneracy. Less than a month after the attack on George Pratt, he attacked six-year-old Harry Austin. Harry was stripped and beaten, but this time Pomeroy produced a knife and stabbed the child under each arm and between his shoulders. He then tried to cut off the boy's penis, but was disturbed and fled the scene before completing the task.

Six days later, he lured Joseph Kennedy, 7, to a marsh. He forced the boy to kneel and ordered him to recite a profane version of the Lord's Prayer. When Joseph refused, Pomeroy slashed his face with a knife. Less than a week later, he tied five-year-old Robert Gould to a post near railroad tracks in South Boston. He beat and slashed at the boy, but was startled into fleeing by approaching railroad workers. This time, at least, the police had a more substantial clue as young Robert described his attacker's milky eye.

With this detail in hand, the police began a search of Boston's schools. On September 21, 1872, they arrived at Jesse Pomeroy's school with one of his victims, Joe Kennedy, in tow. Unfortunately, Kennedy was unable to identify Pomeroy as his assailant.

However, on the way home from school that day, Pomeroy walked into the South Boston police station where detectives were questioning Kennedy. Why he did this is unknown, but psychopaths have been known to engage in games with the police, and perhaps that was his intention. If so, the move backfired badly. When Joe Kennedy again spotted Pomeroy, he immediately pointed him out as the boy who had attacked him. Pomeroy took flight but was captured half a block away.

Locked in a cell and subjected to an intimidating round of questioning, Jesse stubbornly stuck to his guns and protested his innocence. Eventually the officers gave up and contacted his mother to inform her that he was in custody. Pomeroy was left in a dark cell until midnight when officers returned to resume their interrogation. This time they threatened him with a 100-year prison term unless he confessed. Pomeroy then broke down and admitted the attacks.

Justice followed swiftly. Pomeroy was in front of a magistrate the next day, where each of his victims stepped forward to recount how he'd attacked them. Ruth Pomeroy took the stand in her son's defense, tearfully describing him as a hardworking and obedient boy. The magistrate was unmoved. He sentenced Pomeroy to the Reformatory at Westborough, there to remain until he was 18.

As with most houses of reformation in that era, Westborough was a tough institution where the strong preyed on the weak. However, Pomeroy's reputation went before him. Youngsters cowered in fear in his presence, while the older boys largely left him alone. He quickly learned that his only way to get out before his 18th birthday was to become a model inmate. So exemplary was his behavior that he was made a hall monitor, a position he loved for the authority it gave him.

Meanwhile, Ruth Pomeroy was working tirelessly to free her son. She began a letter-writing campaign, addressing the board of overseers at Westborough and anyone else who might help her case. But her insistence that Jesse had been falsely accused alienated the authorities. When he was eventually released, it was not because they believed his protestations of innocence, but because they concluded that he had been rehabilitated.

And so, after serving less than eighteen months for his horrendous crimes, Jesse Pomeroy was released from Westborough Reformatory into the care of his mother. Two young children would pay a horrific price for his liberty.

At the time, Ruth Pomeroy ran a dressmaking shop while her older son, Charles, operated a newsstand, both businesses located close to their home on the 300 block of Broadway in South Boston. Six weeks after his release, on March 18, 1874, Jesse was sweeping the floor in his mother's shop. Also present was Rudolph Kohr, a local boy who sometimes ran errands for the Pomeroys.

At around 8 p.m., ten-year-old Katie Curran entered the store and asked if they had any notepads in stock. Jesse said that they had only one left, which he'd let Katie have at a discount as it had an ink spot on the cover. He then asked Rudolph to go to the butcher's shop for some scraps of meat to feed the cats. Rudolph agreed and left the store.

Once he was gone, Jesse told Katie to come with him down to the cellar to fetch the notebook. Innocently, the girl followed, but they'd barely made it to the foot of the stairs when Pomeroy grabbed her, got an arm around her neck and slit her throat, almost severing her head. He then cut open her dress and undergarments and launched a savage postmortem attack on her abdomen and genitals, stabbing and slashing. His bloodlust apparently sated, he dragged the girl's body across the cellar floor and hid it behind the water closet, covering it with rubble. Hearing his brother enter the store, Jesse quickly washed his hands and ran upstairs. He then went about his workday as though nothing had happened.

Katie Curran was expected home by 8:30. When she didn't return, her mother launched a frantic search. Her first point of call was Tobin's General Store. The proprietor confirmed that Katie had been there, but that he'd sent her to Pomeroy's. The news caused Mrs. Curran to panic. She'd heard of Jesse Pomeroy and his misdeeds. She went immediately to the police. However, the precinct captain assured her that Jesse Pomeroy was not a threat to her daughter. "He's been completely rehabilitated," Captain Henry Dyer said. "Besides, he only hurt little boys. He's never attacked a girl."

A day passed with no sign of Katie. Then Rudolph Kohr came forward and told Mary Curran he'd seen Katie in the Pomeroy's store. Again Mrs. Curran went to the police, although the response she got was far from enthusiastic. "The Kohr boy is a known liar," Captain Dyer told her, although at Mrs. Curran's insistence, he did agree to send an officer to the store to carry out a search. It turned up nothing untoward.

As the weeks passed, Jesse Pomeroy must have thought he'd got away with the murder. He began trying to lure children again, promising them money, candy or trips to the circus. Most of the kids had been warned about him and were wise enough to refuse his offers. However, he almost succeeded with five-year-old Harry Field. Having lured the child by offering him five cents, Pomeroy was leading him through the streets by the hand when he encountered another teenager from the neighborhood. Knowing Pomeroy's reputation, the youth insisted that he release Harry. As the two of them argued, Harry pulled free of Pomeroy's grasp and ran for it. Without doubt, the unnamed youth saved Harry's life that day. Pomeroy's next victim would not be so lucky.

Horace Millen was a cherub-faced four-year-old, the beloved youngest son of the Millen family who had recently moved into the area. On a chill, early spring morning, Horace managed to beg a couple of pennies from his mother to spend at the corner bakery. Along the way, he encountered an older boy who asked where he was headed. The two then set off for the bakery together. The older boy was Jesse Pomeroy.

At the bakery, Horace bought a small cake, which he shared with his new friend. Jesse then suggested a trip to the nearby harbor to see the ships, and Horace was happy to go along. The two set off together, walking hand in hand.

A number of witnesses saw them that day: one leaving the bakery together; another wandering near some railroad tracks; another crossing a marshy area known as the "cow pasture." The last person besides Jesse Pomeroy to see Horace Millen alive was a beachcomber who spotted them from a distance. He later told police that the older boy kept looking furtively over his shoulder as though someone were following them.

Eventually, Pomeroy found a small copse of trees that would afford some privacy. "Let's rest for a minute," he told Horace. Then, as the toddler sat, Pomeroy produced his knife and pounced on him. He slashed at the boy's throat releasing a spray of blood. But Horace wasn't killed, he fought bravely for his life, sustaining numerous wounds to his hands as Pomeroy slashed and stabbed at him. Eventually, though, the boy succumbed to his injuries. Now in a frenzy, Pomeroy stabbed at his victim, raining blows on his chest and genitals. One wound punctured an eye and Pomeroy then tried to castrate the boy, mutilating his scrotum.

At around 4 p.m. that same day, two brothers playing along the beach found Horace's body. The boys ran for help and encountered a couple of hunters who went for the police.

Horace had, of course, already been reported missing by now, so it didn't take long before he was identified. It did not take long either for police to identify a suspect. The crime perfectly fit Pomeroy's M.O., and with the number of witnesses who had seen him with Horace, he was soon in custody.

The evidence against him, including eyewitness reports, a bloody knife found in his possession, a boot print left at the scene, and fresh scratches on his face and arms, was overwhelming. But still Pomeroy continued to protest his innocence. It was only when the police insisted that he accompany them to the funeral parlor to view Horace's brutalized corpse that he cracked.

"I'm sorry I did it," he wept. "Please don't tell my mother."

Pomeroy's arrest was massive news along the east coast. The media dubbed him "The Boy Fiend," and plastered their front pages with lurid stories about his family, past crimes and confession, much of it wildly exaggerated and sensationalized.

Pomeroy, meanwhile, had recanted his confession. When he took the stand at the coroner's inquest, he denied any involvement in Horace's death. The evidence against him, however, was strong enough to warrant a charge of first-degree murder. And that meant that 14-year-old Jesse Pomeroy was facing the death penalty.

Meanwhile, things were not going well for Ruth Pomeroy and her son Charles. In the wake of Jesse's arrest, their businesses faced a widespread boycott from the locals, and eventually they were forced to shut down the store. Their former co-tenant decided to take over the premises and, in the process of refurbishing the cellar, workmen discovered the remains of Katie Curran, now in an advanced state of decomposition.

It was obvious who had committed this atrocity. The only question was whether Ruth and Charles Pomeroy had known about the murder. They were taken into custody, as much for their own protection as to determine whether they were involved. Jesse was able to clear that up. He'd killed Katie, he admitted, but his mother and brother knew nothing about the murder. Jesse Pomeroy now stood accused of two murders. And it looked likely that he would become the youngest person ever executed in the state of Massachusetts.

The trial began on December 8, 1874, and concluded in February 1875 with a guilty verdict. The sentence was death. Only an act of mercy by Governor William Gaston could save Jesse Pomeroy from the gallows. Fortunately for Pomeroy, Gaston was reluctant to execute someone so young. Unfortunately for him, Gaston was soon out of office, his successor, Alexander Rice, elected largely because he promised to hang Jesse Pomeroy. Rice would soon renege on that promise, commuting Pomeroy's sentence to life in prison. There was one proviso – the sentence was to be served in solitary confinement.

Jesse Pomeroy would remain behind bars for 58 years, most of it in solitary. He died at Bridgewater prison farm in 1931, at the age of 73.

For more True Crime books by Robert Keller please visit

http://bit.ly/kellerbooks

Printed in Great Britain
by Amazon

10087916R00092